JOURNAL OF A REVOLUTIONARY WAR WOMAN

IN THEIR OWN WORDS

Journal of a REVOLUTIONARY WAR Woman

Judith E. Greenberg
Helen Carey McKeever

FRANKLIN WATTS
A DIVISION OF GROLIER PUBLISHING
New York / London / Hong Kong / Sydney
Danbury, Connecticut

to Aunt Eve and Uncle Herb Blum
—JEG
to my cousin Ralph Morton and his wife, Miriam
—HCM

Photographs copyright ©: Bettmann Archive: pp. 2, 54, 59, 64, 77, 111; North Wind Picture Archives: pp. 14, 16, 27, 117; Stock Montage, Inc.: p. 57; New York Public Library Picture Collection: pp. 10, 42, 43, 55, 79, 121,122; Brooklyn Historical Society: p. 70; New York Public Library Rare Book Division: p. 34; Library of Congress: pp. 19, 48, 62, 112, 115; Nassau County Museum Collection, Long Island Studies Institute: p. 22; The Metropolitan Museum of Art, Bequest of Charles A. Munn, 1924: p. 38; Courtesy, Winterthur Museum: p. 97.

Library of Congress Cataloging-in-Publication Data

Greenberg, Judith E.
     Journal of a revolutionary war woman / by Judith E Greenberg and Helen Carey McKeever.
          p. cm. — (In their own words)
     An annotated personal account drawn from: Personal recollections of the American Revolution / by Lydia Minturn Post. 1859.
     Includes bibliographical references and index.
     Summary: entries from the journal of Mary Titus Post written during the American Revolution are presented with background information to help explain their historical context.
     ISBN 0-531-11259-4
     1. Post, Mary Titus—Diaries—Juvenile literature 2. United States— History—Revolution, 1775–1783—Personal narratives— Juvenile literature. 3 United States—History—Revolution, 1775– 1783—Women—Juvenile literature. 4. Women—United States— Diaries—Juvenile literature. [1. Post, Mary Titus. 2. United States— History—Revolution, 1775–1783—Personal narratives. 3. Women— Biography. 4. Diaries.] I. McKeever, Helen Carey. II. Post, Lydia Minturn. Personal recollections of the American Revolution. III. Title. IV. Series.
E275.P86G74 1996
973.3'8—dc20
[B]   95-46727 CIP AC

CONTENTS

INTRODUCTION
THE MYSTERY
IN HISTORY

HOW DO HISTORIANS KNOW about events that happened hundreds of years ago? They look for and collect evidence to learn the truth about people, places, and events. Evidence is anything that offers information and can contribute to a conclusion. It probably won't surprise you to discover that often there is disagreement about some conclusions. In order to uncover the truth, historians gather all the facts they can find, and as much evidence as possible, and then draw their conclusions. In a sense, historians are like detectives who piece together clues in their search for the truth. But, as human beings, historians have their own experiences and opinions and these affect how they interpret certain events. Therefore, two historians may come to different conclusions about where, how, and why things happened.

For example, some historians wondered for years about the exact cause of Napoleon Bonaparte's death. He died in exile on the island of St. Helena in 1821, a time when few scientific tests existed that could help explain or reconstruct the cause of his death. A Swedish scientist and historian named Sven Forshufvud, who had a special interest in toxicology (the study of poisons and their effects), thought he had the answer. He suggested that Napoleon had been poisoned, probably by someone close to him during his exile. Forshufvud theorized that arsenic, administered in small doses over a period of time, could have caused the changes in Napoleon's health and appearance noted when he died.

Forshufvud examined primary source documents, including Napoleon's autopsy reports and the memoirs of Louis Marchand, who was Napoleon's servant and companion on St. Helena. He charted the changes in Napoleon's health that seemed consistent with arsenic poisoning. Forshufvud knew that traces of arsenic remain in strands of a person's hair. Fortunately, saving locks of hair as keepsakes was a common practice in the nineteenth century. Forshufvud tested a tiny sample of Napoleon's hair, and was able to detect the presence of arsenic. He used this as evidence to prove his theory. However, other scientists were not convinced and countered Forshufvud's theory with their own. They said that the hair samples also contained large amounts of antimony—a chemical used in many nineteenth-century medicines. They claimed this was evidence that Napoleon had suffered from stomach cancer, which would account for the physical changes observers noted. Then some scientists found evidence that suggested that the arsenic traces in Napoleon's hair could have come from his home environment. The wallpaper in his home was painted with a green pigment that contained arsenic. Vapors from this common nineteenth-century paint could cause weakness, nausea, and enlarged limbs, all of which Napoleon exhibited at the time of his death. To this day, the cause of Napoleon's death remains not fully clear. The mystery may never be solved.

Personal Recollections of the American Revolution. A Private Journal. Prepared From Authentic Domestic Records by Lydia Minturn Post. Edited by Sidney Barclay presents some tantalizing mysteries, too. The book was first published in 1859. The main mystery about it is: Who wrote the recollections and who lived them? We know that "Sidney Barclay" was a writing pseudonym used by Lydia Minturn Post, who also wrote under the name of Grace Barclay. In fact, in 1867 Lydia reissued *Personal Recollections,* this time under the title *Grace Barclay's Diary.* It was the same book. No one seems to know Lydia's reason for doing this.

Who was Lydia Minturn Post? According to Quaker records, she was born in the early 1800s and was the daughter of Henry Post and Mary Minturn. Her grandparents on her father's side were Henry Post and Mary Titus, residents of the town of Westbury, Long Island, during the American Revolution. The village of Westbury is the principal setting for *Personal Recollections* and its inhabitants are the people whose lives are recorded in history and in Lydia Minturn Post's publication.

Whose story does *Personal Recollections* present? Who is the woman who is recalling the American Revolution and the siege of Long Island? For the last one hundred or so years, readers, historians, and the Library of Congress have accepted the book as the nonfiction journal of a woman named Lydia Minturn Post. However, the genealogical and time-frame references point toward Mary Titus Post. It is not known why Lydia did not state that *Personal Recollections* was based on her grandmother's story; however, she never denied it, either. In the full title of the book, Lydia states that she edited the *Recollections.*

There are people who think a mystery still exists. One author, Sarah Buck, writes in a recent article in the *Long Island Historical Journal,* (Vol 7, No. 2, pp. 191–204), that

*The Battle of Long Island: "The Retreat of
the Americans across Gowanus Creek"*

Personal Recollections is actually an "embellished, if not a completely fictionalized, diary of life in the Revolution reconstructed from an antebellum perspective." Ms. Buck discusses details such as the location of the parsonage and some of the names of people and places mentioned in the book. She feels that the language and some of the political views represent the nineteenth century (when Lydia lived) rather than the eighteenth century (Mary's time period.) Ms. Buck's article illustrates the problems of fact-finding and interpretation that are part of the historian's job.

From our search for answers to the historical mystery

of *Personal Recollections*, we conclude that Lydia Minturn Post was the granddaughter of Mary Titus Post. Lydia tells of her grandmother's historical experience, but she sometimes combines names and personalities of two or more people into one person and moves locations of houses and buildings. Did Lydia make these changes on purpose, or were family stories handed down that way? It is not clear. What is clear, as Lydia says in her title, is that she was working from authentic domestic records—diaries, letters, family recollections, Quaker church records, and other primary source materials—which, being written by people, undoubtedly contained some faulty statements, or errors. Misinformation and the distance of two generations also contribute to the varying viewpoints about *Personal Recollections* and the haze surrounding the story.

Personal Recollections is the story of a woman who sacrifices along with her family, and is propelled on a journey into danger and privation by the events of the American Revolution. Her journal records the sufferings and losses, the hopes and grievances, the fears and sacrifices of her family and neighbors during the long years of war.

Few pleasures can compare with reading original diaries, journals, and letters. However, the reading of a diary or journal or personal letters requires a bit of work because they cannot be read like an ordinary story. In the usual story there is a beginning, a middle, and an end. But in a journal or letters, the thoughts are often random and spontaneous. The writer may move from topic to topic within a sentence or paragraph, and may sometimes let days and weeks pass without writing much.

In reading *Personal Recollections* it is helpful to remember that the writer was putting down on paper what she might have said in a real conversation. She leaves out some details about people and events because she already knows the names, places, and particulars. But for today's reader, we have provided information to help clarify this personal chronicle of the American Revolution. As an example, in one entry she tells her husband about General Mercer's death. Her husband was most likely on the same battlefield as Mercer and knew all about the battle at Princeton, thus she doesn't provide specific details. To overcome the lack of historical details in this entry, and in others in *Personal Recollections*, we have attempted to fill in the blanks for you.

As you begin reading *Personal Recollections* you will see that the language is flowery and very different from today's style. But much as the old-fashioned clothes and hairstyles in an old movie become less strange as the characters gain our interest, so the journal's style gradually seems less odd as the reader is drawn into the story.

We have organized this book into chapters, each containing portions of *Personal Recollections* and historical notes. Woven throughout the chapters are the threads of four major themes: The woman's struggle to survive the war with her family, neighbors, and nation intact and safe; her deep love of country and freedom; her admiration of courage; and her belief that decency and kindness will prevail over cruelty. Through the diary, we hear a woman's gentle and pleasant voice making clear her feelings about the extraordinary times in which she lived.

Mary Titus Post lived in a time and place that was controlled by an enemy. Writing letters and keeping a journal may have given her a sense of control over the enormous changes that were taking place before her eyes. To put her feelings into words and know that her husband would read them and sympathize must have comforted her. Through these words we see emerging a strong woman, a caring mother, a dutiful wife and daughter. That is what makes her journal compelling—it is about the persistence of hope in the midst of personal danger and the possibility of defeat for her country.

THE STORY
BEGINS

THE WORDS YOU ARE ABOUT TO READ begin a journal recounting a growing crisis in America that was to lead to the American Revolution. The journal and chronicle of the war begins and ends at the parsonage, the Long Island, New York, home of Mary Titus Post's father. Long Island in the eighteenth century was a world of tiny villages surrounded by small isolated farms and by the elegant manor estates of wealthy, powerful families. Long Island industry included sawmills, gristmills, and shipyards.

In small homes and on large estates, Long Islanders were devoutly religious people with close family ties. Mary counted among her friends, her Quaker neighbors as well as prominent Anglican and Dutch families.

By the time she writes her first words in the journal, Long Islanders had already reacted to several important events in the war for independence. Island patriots had protested the Stamp Act and after the Boston Tea Party, most Islanders gave up drinking tea and agreed to end trade with England. While most Long Islanders supported

An eighteenth-century Long Island manor house

the Continental Congress and the Declaration of Independence, Loyalists did not, and they responded differently to the news of Lexington and Concord and the Battle of Bunker Hill. Rebel islanders were joyous; Loyalists were outraged. In the midst of this turmoil, the British forces were able to make New York City their headquarters and capture Long Island on August 27, 1776. *Personal Recollections* begins as the war sweeps over the whole of Long Island and the Colonial army.

During the eight long years of war, the farmers and the residents of Long Island were forced to provide huge quantities of animals, food, and wood to the British army at prices set by the army. If they refused to hand over horses and cows, firewood, hay, straw, corn, and oats, the provisions were confiscated and the farmers were threatened with imprisonment. Throughout the war, Long Island served as a British troop depot. The island swarmed with enemy troops, especially during the winter months as the soldiers settled in to rest after the summer campaigns. And if British occupation was not bad enough, the Island also had to contend with lawless men, both Loyalist and Rebel, who sailed into the Island's harbors and came ashore to rob and murder.

Military occupation brought many outrages against the local civilian population. Churches were often used as granaries, their pews burned for fuel or used as building materials, and church sanctuaries used as barracks and stables. In one Long Island town British troops constructed a fort in the middle of a cemetery and used tombstones as bases for fireplaces and bake ovens. Anglican churches were generally left alone by the British, as their Anglican or Church of England congregations usually sided with England during the war.

Those civilians and others who wished the union with England to continue were called Tories or Loyalists. Americans who favored the revolution were known as Rebels. Families, church congregations, and whole villages and towns were splintered into Loyalist and Rebel groups when the war and the occupying troops came to Long Island.

After the British occupied Long Island the citizens were forced to sign loyalty oaths to His Majesty King George III. They promised to be faithful subjects of the king and not aid the rebels in any way. Some people signed willingly; some signed knowing they wouldn't honor it, and still others chose to leave Long Island and cross into Connecticut where they could fight on the American side.

The Americans were poorly prepared for the war. They lacked experienced officers, organization, ammunition, and even uniforms. However, the colonials did have one or two important advantages. They were defending their own country and fighting in their own communities. The British were strangers to the land. Also, when the Americans began their revolt, Great Britain was committed to other skirmishes in Europe and was hampered by a short supply of trained officers and soldiers. Thus Britain was not the overwhelming force it would normally have been. And as

I Do hereby certify, that *Elihu Rayner* Aged 26 of Southampton Township, has voluntarily swore before me, to bear Faith and true Allegiance to his Majesty King George the Third; and that he will not, directly or indirectly, openly or secretly, aid, abet, counsel, shelter or conceal, any of his Majesty's Enemies, and those of his Government, or molest or betray the Friends of Government; but that he will behave himself peaceably and quietly, as a faithful Subject of his Majesty and his Government. Given under my Hand on Long-Island, this 22 *Sept,* —————— 1778.

Wm Tryon Gov.

A loyalty oath

the war progressed, the Americans gained experience and began winning battles.

From the start, both sides had trouble getting enough soldiers. At its peak in 1776, Washington's army numbered 18,000 soldiers. But soldiers often served for only a few months at a time. Most colonists were against having a large standing army, so the revolt became a militiaman's war, with groups of men organizing themselves under the leadership of local officers. Then, when the battle was won or the danger of invasion was over, the men went back to their farms and families.

Keeping the men in the militia was a constant problem. Wives often wrote to their husbands in the Continental Army and begged them to come home because the family farm was failing and their children were starving. During the winter at Valley Forge, General George Washington issued orders to keep women out of the camp because he was worried about wives who might find their husbands and plead with them to come home. Washington and other colonial officers grew discouraged at having only a few well-trained soldiers on hand for important battles. Washington had about 17,000 troops under his command

16

when the war ended, and this number included French soldiers and sailors.

After the war was over, historians began to understand why the British also had difficulty in getting enough soldiers to fight in this war. In the first place, the fighting was taking place 3,000 miles away from home. Many Englishmen felt that the colonies were too far away and that their lives weren't affected by a group of renegade colonists. In addition, many British soldiers sympathized with the American cause and didn't want to fight. For these reasons and also because many British soldiers were fighting elsewhere in the world, the king of England was forced to hire soldiers, most of whom came from the German state of Hesse to fight in the colonies. But at the time, Mary had no way of knowing that the British faced these difficulties. To her the British seemed unbeatable as they quickly captured Long Island and Manhattan, causing her to fear for the safety of her family and her country.

Shortly after her husband left to serve in the army, Mary and her three children went to live with her father in the church parsonage on Long Island. In this quiet place she hoped to find peace and safety. On the front porch of her father's home, Mary sews, learns the news that her father gathers from his walks in the neighborhood, reads her husband's letters, and answers his inquiries either in her letters to him or in her journal.

The first words to appear in *Personal Recollections* are those of Mary's husband, Edward, urging her to put her thoughts and feelings on paper. Perhaps he felt that the journal would keep the two of them close during the time he was away fighting the war.

Write from thy heart, Mary, from the inmost recesses of it, that I may look into it, as it loves, hopes, thinks, fears, that, though absent, thou mayest be near, and that thy troubles, thy cares, may be shared, though not alleviated, by one whom thou lovest, and who loves thee.

The next words in *Personal Recollections* are a reply to her husband's wish that she put her thoughts on paper. Thus she begins in September 1776 with these words:

The request shall be granted; each day a page in the journal, or a letter to my husband.

Mary refers to General George Washington and his army's escape from a trap set by the British General William Howe at Brooklyn. Howe's army had the Americans surrounded but under the cover of a heavy fog, Washington was able to sneak his army out of a near-disastrous situation and back to Manhattan, mainly because Howe did not follow up his advantage. She next describes her father's parsonage to Edward.

September, 1776

Still at the Parsonage with my three precious children; already heart-weary at your absence, but striving to keep up courage. Today received intelligence of the unfortunate affair of Brooklyn. What a skillful movement was that of General Washington—a wonderful retreat! The enemy so near that the sound of their pickaxes and shovels could be heard! It is a new proof of his cool forethought and judgment. The heavy fog seemed to fall providentially. May we not accept it as an omen that our leader is the favored of Heaven?

In this quiet nook where we had hoped to find peace and safety, we shall have disturbance, fear, and danger; since the enemy have possession of the island, there can be no doubt of it, but to some extent my father's neutral stand and sacred profession will protect us.

An early engraving depicts the evacuation of Washington's troops after their defeat at the Battle of Long Island, August 27, 1776.

As we have moved to this place, dear Edward, since you left us, I think it will be agreeable to you to have some little description of it. It is a low-roofed, Dutch style of a house, with its gable to the road; white-washed and covered with sweetbriar and creeping vines of many kinds. And my father has planted the ivy, which came from his dear Old England. It grows slowly, and the children love to pick its glossy leaves, and carry them to grandpa. At the sight of them, his heart of tenderness reverts to early days; he tells them of the old castles, and gray ruins it [the ivy] mantles over the sea, and of the one which overgrew the cottage where he was born. The thoughts of my dear, honored parent remind me of a brave old tree torn up by its roots, and transplanted into a foreign soil. It may not die, but it has a sickly appearance, and its leaves have lost their living green, and are pale and yellow.

The front door opens into a hall of moderate size. On the right is the parlor; back of it is my father's study, while on the other side is the dining room and the bedroom, and in the wing the kitchen. The rooms above are spacious and convenient, the windows at the end being large, admitting air and light. Across the front of the dwelling runs the piazza or covered porch. Here we sit and sew, and talk, and read.

In other entries Mary's thoughts are obviously in turmoil as she jumps from a description of a peaceful little pond next to the parsonage to her worry over the outcome of the war and her steadfast support of the colonial cause, to a defense of her father's wish that the British prevail and are able put down the rebellious colonies. She is an ardent patriot, but she does her best to see her father's viewpoint and hopes that her husband, Edward, will, too.

There are two homesteads besides our own which border the Pond. [Probably Westbury Pond] It is a beautiful little sheet of water. My father often says it would, in the old countries, be called a lake, tarn, or some other pretty name. Well, it would not any more enliven *our* prospect as it sparkles in the sun, and grows dark and shadowy in the twilight. Nor would

Charley [Mary's son] delight the more to sail his mimic ship, or paddle the canoe upon its bosom, that he does now the livelong day. There is a small island [possibly Goose Island] in the center, which is called after the silly birds [Canadian geese and other wading birds] which dearly love to swim the water, land thereon, flap and dry their wings and scream their pleasure.

Long Island is an island that forms the southeastern part of New York. It stretches eastward from the mouth of the Hudson River for nearly 120 miles. It varies in width from 12 to 23 miles. Although *Personal Recollections* does not say specifically where the parsonage was located on Long Island, there are sufficient clues and place names given by her to determine that it was in the settlement of Westbury, which was named after a county in England.

My father tells me the news, which he gathers in his walks in the neighborhood; and I read to him portions of your letters, which indeed is but seldom, because they are so few. His breast is, I think, agitated by contending emotions. He is attached to the land of his adoption, and can sympathize in her distress, but naturally his first, his dearest affections, were given to the land of his birth. Can we censure this? Call it infatuation, blindness? Oh, no! I honor my father for the sentiment. Do not condemn it, Edward. *We* love this, our native land, the native country of my mother, of both your parents. Her cause seems to us a righteous one. She is overtaxed, oppressed, insulted; my father feels this, he is indignant at it. Yet, in his character of ambassador of Christ, follower of the Crucified, as well as by nature's instinct, he *hates* the sin, while he *loves* the sinner. They seem (the English) the foes of our own household to him; brother lifting up sword against brother, in unnatural warfare, which he prays may speedily come to an end!

21

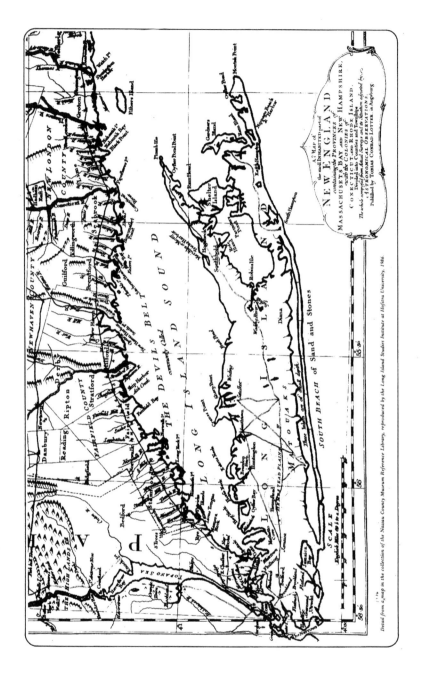

A colonial period map of the province of New York. Westbury, the likely setting for Personal Recollections, is located near the initial L of Long Island.

Detail from a map in the collection of the Nassau County Museum Reference Library, reproduced by the Long Island Studies Institute at Hofstra University, 1986.

Mary worried constantly about her nation and whether or not the colonies can win the war. She was a passionate supporter of the revolution and was convinced of the rightness of the American cause. She was not alone in her fears and her hopes for the struggling country. Of the two and a half million people who lived in the colonies, almost half were women. Many fine ladies, servant girls, and middle-class women were as supportive of the revolution as Mary was—and as worried.

December 17, 1776

No public news this many a day. My womanish fears, as you name them, get the better of me. The disparity between the contending parties is so immense. The mother country, the first maritime power on the globe; her great wealth, vast resources, well disciplined armies, experienced military and naval commanders. What have the Colonies to oppose such an array of means and power?

Inexperienced officers; raw, undisciplined troops; scant arms and munitions of war; small revenue; few armed ships!

Be still, my anxious heart! "All things are possible to them that believe." "By faith we can move mountains." Mountains they appear when we look at human means, which seem utterly inadequate. But "the race is not to the swift, nor the battle to the strong." What is this struggle of the Colonies? Is it a war of aggression, of cupidity, of conquest, of fierce passion, for tyranny and despotic sway? No—it is the noble endeavor, the strong purpose, founded in inalienable right, to throw off a galling yoke unjustly and perseveringly imposed. It is the cry of humanity against oppression, usurped power, insolence, and rapacity. Will it prevail, or will it be smothered?

2
WAR COMES TO THE NEIGHBORHOOD

PERSONAL RECOLLECTIONS begins a tale of exciting, if trying times. Some experiences Mary saw or heard about were mild; others were vicious and terrible. During a war there are often some people who roam the countryside robbing and burning, and threatening local citizens. The roving bands of thugs that Mary tells about were made up of regular British soldiers or Hessians, and deserters from both the British and colonial armies, as well as ordinary thieves and bullies. The Long Islanders called these vicious marauders by various names, most often Redcoats, Cowboys, Runners, Skinners, and Robbers. The gangs roamed the neutral ground, the area between the American and British armies on Long Island, taking the property of anyone they captured. The patriot gangs were called Skinners and the Loyalist gangs were Cowboys.

Some colonists defended themselves by firing on these ruffians. Others were too frightened to stand firm and the hoodlums were able to rob them and get away. *Personal Recollections* describes attacks Mary learned about and the heroism of the local people, especially the unarmed women and children.

Saturday, October, 1776

I have to-day to record deeds of horror, and of heroism, seldom equalled.

The house of Mr. Wilmot Oakley, near Cold Spring, was attacked last night. He had long expected, and was prepared to meet the attack, being proverbially brave and powerful.

The robbers forced open the front door, and entered the sitting-room, adjoining Mr. and Mrs. Oakley's bedroom. Two loaded guns stood in the corner of the room. The robbers were armed with pistols and swords. On opening the door, Mr. Oakley saw three men, one of whom called out, "Surrender, and give up your money!" Not he. They had this time met their equal in daring— the man to fight it out, and the woman too!

Mr. Oakley fired his gun, and one of the intruders his pistol, which triflingly grazed the ear of Mr. Oakley. He handed his wife the [first] gun, and took from her [another] loaded one; fired it off, and his man fell. While she reloaded, he warded the other two of the rascals off with his gun in his hand. He then took the gun again loaded by Mrs. Oakley, fired, and the second man reeled and fell. The other man, seeing one of his comrades dead and the other fallen, ran out of the house. Mr. Oakley (with his gun reloaded) after him, fired at him as he was running on the road. [In] The morning traces of blood were seen in the road and on the fence, so that there is little doubt that he was wounded, though he escaped.

I am glad to say every effort was made to save the life of the robber, who lay in a dreadful condition on the floor of the parlor, but it proved unavailing. He followed his companion in wickedness before the light of day.

Sunday, December, 1776

The church was opened for divine service today. It was unusually solemn. Many officers and soldiers attended. They were serious and attentive.

Our beautiful clover field is trampled upon and ruined. My dear father was so fond of its luxuriance! When the dew was on it, the air came laden with delicious odor, regaling us when we sat on the porch. The children used to make posies and wreaths of the large red and white flowers, and often expatiated fondly and gratefully on the rich feast preparing for the horse and brindle cow, by Him who "giveth the early and the latter rain." The clover seed came from England. While in church a company of fifty horsemen rode into the field, and quite cropped and destroyed it. I have persuaded my father to make complaint to Colonel Wurms; but there is no redress.

(Redress means to have someone listen to your complaint and see that you are repaid.) Mary's father had no luck in getting the British Colonel Wurms to stop his men from destroying personal and church property. Mary writes next of other alarming episodes happening to families living near the parsonage. Most of these families were members of the Religious Society of Friends, or Quakers.

Quakerism developed in England in the 1600s and because Quakers were persecuted for their beliefs, many English Quakers emigrated to America. Quakers reject war and stress peace. Many Quakers sought to avoid confrontation with their British masters and ignored the revolution as best they could. Other Quakers, although they refused to fight, were quietly sympathetic to the rebel cause. Mary's Quaker neighbors reacted to the intrusions of the Cowboys, Runners, and Skinners in one of two ways. Some patiently accepted what was happening to them; others found peaceful ways to outwit intruders who forced their way into their homes. In her letters to her husband,

*Quaker immigrants brought their
message of peace to the colonies.*

Mary voices her pride in the bravery exhibited by Long
Island residents.

Tuesday, November, 1776

Edith Pattison came over to the Parsonage today
for the first time. She is a sweet young Quakeress.
Her pure, lovely, and attractive looks are indeed winning. She wore a silvery drab poplin. The sleeves came
just above the elbow, a little white frill below. Her arms
are round and white. She wears always a neat gauze
cap. It is thought unseemly in their Society that a

young woman's head should be uncovered. She is very fair, though her hair and eyes are dark. Her aspect is mild, gentle and pensive. I can describe to you the outline of Edith's features, but not the spiritual expression of her face. She is made a perfect lady of by her eight doting brothers. They will fetch, and carry, and run for their beautiful sister, as though she were a queen. And when you look at her, you do not think it strange, her air and mien are so serene, and dignity sits enthroned upon her brow.

Doubtless when you read my Journal, penned for your eye, you will exclaim, "How *could* she calmly write these details in stirring times like these?" But remember, Edward, I must be occupied about something. It beguiles the attention, and keeps off sad thoughts of you, which, when I give way to them, rend my heart. My precious father's peace is disturbed, and even the dear children appear to participate in the foreboding gloom.

Wednesday, November, 1776

Charles accompanied John Harris home from school, with my permission, last night. He returned this morning, with a story of the night, which he related to me in breathless excitement.

A family living a mile from us [the W.___ family] were quietly sitting together in the evening, when a noise was heard at the door like that of a sharp instrument thrust into it. On opening the door, there stood a redcoat with his sabre in his hand, which he had stuck into the wood an inch or two. He was backed by a dozen men. They pushed their way in, and were very unruly, rummaging and ransacking every drawer and closet; but the family had long before taken the precaution to place all their valuables and money in a small room, which opened out of a common sitting-room, putting a large cupboard before the door, which covered it entirely; so that the Hessians quartered there last winter never discovered the existence of the room. A cunning device.

The redcoats, highly enraged at finding nothing, began to threaten terrible things if they did not divulge the hiding place. Mr. W. told them that if they dared do any violence he would report them to their commanding officer, whereupon they actually went into the kitchen, kindled some light wood, came out and set a burning brand at each corner of the house. The family were exceedingly alarmed. In great terror, Sarah, the youngest daughter, rushed out. She is famed through all the north side for her comeliness. I can well imagine that she must have appeared to them like a lovely apparition, with her flashing eyes and glowing cheeks. The ringleader, astonished, stood with his torch in his hand, gazing at her.

At length he said, "Angel!"

"Stop, I entreat you," said Sarah. His looks were riveted upon her in ardent admiration, which embarrassed her.

"I will, on one condition," said he.

"What is it?" said she.

"Will you grant it?"

"If I can," replied Sarah.

"It is that you will allow me to kiss you."

"Oh, if that is all," said her father, "comply, my daughter." So, as she made no resistance, the rough soldier planted a fervent kiss on her lips, and departed.

They found before her baby-house [dollhouse] that the soldiers had stuck the dolls on their bayonets, and railed among themselves and laughed.

It is seldom that a man's house is attacked more than once. Mr Harris had his turn some time ago; therefore, although he saw some suspicious-looking persons lurking about, he feared nothing, and rose before daylight, with the intention of going to the south of the island for salt hay.

Mrs. Harris, however, began to feel uneasy and

The well-equipped and smartly outfitted British Redcoats

timid, from the reports she heard during the day, and persuaded her husband to remain at home. That night passed without disturbance.

About nine o'clock the next evening, a neighbor stopped at the gate in his wagon, and he and Mr. Harris were running over the exciting times and scenes enacting round the country, when they saw a man moving about the fields, and peering out of the edge of the woods now and then. One of the serving women, too, had seen someone about dusk standing close by the woodpile, who vanished on her appearance at the door of the kitchen. In consequence of these signs, Mr. Harris concluded not to retire, but to sit up and keep lights and fires burning about the house.

Charles and the other children were sent to bed, but not to sleep; that was impossible, with their perturbed and excited imaginations.

About twelve o'clock, Mr. Harris being on the lookout, saw a man at a short distance from the house, apparently reconnoitering; he now held a council with his wife and two hired men.

They came to the conclusion that an attack was intended, and that it was time to act; and they determined to leave the house in a body, taking the two guns, loaded, and the money, silver, and small valuables.

Though the next house was full a half mile off, there seemed no other alternative. The poor little frightened children were hurried up and dressed; their fears and cries were hushed, and they were carried downstairs. As quietly as possible all left the house by the back door.

It was a moment of intense anxiety; their hearts beat with dread and terror. With trembling limbs that almost refused to bear them, they slowly and painfully moved on. "Faint, though pursuing," they endeavored to stay their minds above.

At length arrived at Mr. S.'s, another difficulty presented itself. The family would inevitably take them for robbers, and be liable to fire upon them.

In this dilemma Mr. Harris thought it best to go close to the door, and call out his name, trusting that his voice would be recognized, which was the case.

The poor wanderers were warmly received, and provided with comfortable beds, after they had talked over their fright.

The house of Mr. S. has never been attacked, it is so well secured, the doors and windows being lined and barred with iron, which is well known.

A new source of trouble has appeared on the south side—kidnapping Negroes.

The ruffians come in sloops from the Delaware and Maryland country, and landing on the island in the night, they steal the poor creatures while asleep, after the labor of cutting salt meadow grass for their masters. When they get them away, they sell them in the South.

A week since, while men were at work, four persons, in broad day, their faces blackened, and dressed like Negroes, appeared suddenly, each armed with a gun, and before the others could come to the rescue, a man and a boy were forcibly taken, put in a boat, and rowed off to a cutter out at sea. On the deck the villains could be seen putting chains on the poor creatures. I tremble at the thought of the future!

Wednesday, November 24th

Yesterday my indignation was aroused to a high degree. I was sitting in the end of the porch, my father at my side, and little Mary [Marcia], with your letter in her hands, which she was pretending to read, when a loud cry startled us. It seemed to come from neighbor Pattison's, our nearest neighbor. Charles went over, returned, and gave us this account of the affair. It appears that Edmund Pattison was enjoying his noon rest quietly in the barn (he is a noble-looking lad of eighteen, tall and athletic, and of a high spirit), when a light-horseman rode up to the door. "Youngster," said he, "make haste and bestir yourself. Go and assist the driver of the two yoke of oxen there to unload his cart of timber into the road."

Now Edmund had been hard at work with his own hired man, loading the wagon to take the timber to a farmer three miles off, to whom it was sold by his father; the wagon and teams both belonged to the Pattisons.

"Hurry, sir," said the light-horseman.

Edmund firmly replied, "I shall not do it."

"What, sirrah! we shall see who will do it," and drawing his sword, he held it over the head of Edmund, cursing and swearing, and threatening to cut him down, unless he instantly unloaded, and took his team, and helped to carry in it provisions for the army.

With unblanched cheek Edmund Pattison reiterated his denial, and told him to do it himself.

Incensed and enraged beyond measure at such a contempt of orders, it seemed as though the man *must* strike and kill the stubborn boy, who, firm and undaunted, said not a word.

At this time our Charles, who was on the spot, ran to the house and told Mrs. Pattison that "the Britisher was going to kill her Edmund."

Her cry it was that we heard from the porch. She ran to the barn, and begged the soldier to desist. He was more furious than ever, supposing the fear of the mother would induce compliance; she too expostulated with her son, imploring him to assist in unloading the wagon, and save himself from death.

"No fear of death, mother; he dare not touch a hair of my head." The boy was more determined than before, and the soldier more enraged, flourishing his sabre, and swearing that he would be the death of him.

"You dare not. I will report you to your master for this," said Edmund, very boldly. Upon this the light-horseman mounted his horse, and told the brave Edmund once more, that if he did not instantly comply with his request he would cut him in inch pieces!

Edmund coolly walked across the barn floor, armed himself with a huge pitchfork, and took his station in the doorway.

"You cowardly rascal," said he, "take one step towards this floor, and I stab you with my pitchfork!"

His mother could endure the scene no longer; she ran to the house, where she met her husband, and

*Period drawings show an American
rifleman and an infantryman.*

sent him to rescue Edmund. Friend Pattison, a sensible, clear-headed man, rode up, and seeing matters at this high pass on both sides, said to the Britisher, "You know your duty, and have no right to lay a finger on *him*, a non-combatant on neutral ground."

Seeing no signs of relenting, farmer Pattison turned his horse into the direction of the road, and said he would soon see Colonel Wurms, and know *who* had the power to abuse and threaten the farmers of the country in such a manner.

The light-horseman was now alarmed, and thinking it best to get there first, put spurs into his horse, and rode off, uttering awful imprecations.

Thus this time Edmund escaped, though I very much fear his defying fearless spirit may yet cost him dear.

Friday, May, 1777

The farmers have devised a scheme to make known through the neighborhood the presence of the "Runners." They are generally seen lurking about at twilight, spying the points most favorable for attack; if observed, they walk on in an unconcerned manner, whistling or singing. Sometimes they will stop, and inquire the way to some place; suddenly disappearing, they are unexpectedly seen again in the edge of the wood, or from behind a haystack in the field, peering about, terrifying everybody, above all women and children. These signs are not to be mistaken. We are on our guard; the "great gun" with which all are provided, is loaded and fired off. Pop! Pop! go the answering guns for five miles around; each house takes up the alarming tale, and thus it spreads, warning of impending danger, and frightens away the enemy, for *that* time at any rate.

Neighbor Pattison, of his peace-loving spirit, and horror of the "murderous weapon," hath made a large conch shell do the office of a gun; it makes a noble sound, and being close to our vicinity, is a well-known signal. Charles no sooner hears it than he is on the alert; out comes papa's rusty great gun, whose loud report is soon responded to by the whole neighborhood.

November 10, 1777

We were awakened in the dead of night by the sound of the conch shell! Oh, dear husband, I cannot describe to you our consternation. *Our* turn, I thought, had at length come! My first thought was my precious father, old and feeble. . . . The children clung to me with terror. I felt so powerless! Not so Charles, he was bold as a lion—your true son! He promptly got out the great gun, and loaded and fired it, which more than all frightened poor Marcia and Grace. In vain I bade them be pacified; they hid their faces in my gown; the little things trembled with fear. . . .

I persuaded papa to go upstairs; he appeared calm and self-possessed amid our agitation. We now listened intently; not a sound did we hear, but the ticking of the great clock, and our own beating hearts. Again and again we listened; all was still. We remained almost motionless until the dawn of day. The first ray of light was hailed with joy. Charles stole over to neighbor Pattison's expecting, yet dreading to hear a tale of horror, when lo! they greeted him with a great burst of laughter! Now, what think you was the cause, the innocent cause of all this fear and consternation? Little Joseph Pattison! This the story of it:

At noon the elder boys, while standing around the porch, one after the other had been trying the strength of their lungs on the great conch shell, calling the hired men to their dinner. Joseph was eagerly awaiting *his* turn, but it never came at all. The meal was ready, the shell was put away on the high shelf over the door, and dinner over they all went to work again.

Now little Joseph's imagination that night, strongly impressed with his disappointment, ran upon robbers, and the urgent necessity of sounding the shell. Up he sprang, ran downstairs, through two rooms, still asleep, took a chair, reached the conch, and blew it most lustily outside the back door, which roused the household. Down they come, and their astonishment is great to behold the little boy with the seashell in his hand, and though undressed and barefooted, perspiration standing in beads on his forehead from the violent exertion! Would that our frights might always prove as groundless.

Wednesday, 1778

Last night the Runners appeared round a house near West-Town, and were about forcing a door in front when they were discovered. John Rawlins, the owner, sent a Negro upstairs to fire when the word was given. It was a bright moonlight night, and he saw the creatures step up to the door from a window near it with a pane of glass out. In alarm, he looked out for something wherewith to defend himself. Seeing the broom, he took it for want of something better, and ran it through the broken window. It touched the shoulder, and grazed the cheek of one of the villains, who, supposing it to be a loaded gun, cried out piteously, "Oh, heavens, don't kill me!" as though he had never an evil intention towards anyone.

The signal was now given, and the man above fired; they soon scattered, leaving John Rawlins aiming his broomstick through the broken window pane!

In a later letter, Mary tells Edward that things are getting so bad for the Islanders that they have had to form a band of their own to patrol the area and warn households that they may be in danger.

Monday, October, 1780

A dreadful deed was committed last night. Four persons came over from the mainland and attacked

A British view of the American rebel soldier

the house of Richard Albertson. They surrounded it, and one of them knocked loudly at the door. Knowing it to be useless to resist, he got up and opened it. They entered, and with violent gestures told him to hand them all his money. He is considered a wealthy farmer, and they doubtless knew it. He said he had very little in the house, and they would be welcome if they would be satisfied. They thereupon swore furiously, saying they did not believe it, and commenced searching, rummaging drawers, opening closets, and even lifting up the hearthstones, which they have discovered is a favorite hiding place. They found nothing of value. Incensed highly, they commenced swearing and threatening the women, who were excessively terrified. They ordered them to uncord the bedstead, they themselves pulling off the bed clothes. Afraid to disobey, their trembling fingers refused the task. (Mr. Albertson had been put out of the room, so as to play upon the fears of the females.) The ruffians said they wanted the rope to bind him with. They could extort no more by threatening.

They now dragged in the master of the house, and proceeded to put the rope around his neck and tie his hands behind him.

Then the wife and children fell upon their knees and begged the ruffians to spare their father.

Mr. Albertson calmly told them that it was useless to kill him; *that* would not bring money. The wife then offered the wretches all her silver spoons, and twenty dollars in money besides, which they rudely clutched, but demanded more, as violently as before. They now began to abuse his only son, William, a boy of fourteen years, thinking, doubtless, that by exciting the fears and sympathy of the father, the booty would be produced.

The poor man, sorely tried, told the ruffians that money was nothing to him in comparison. If he had it, he would give it to them. What little he *did* possess was let out to his neighbors. Whereupon they began to strike at him with their sabres, knocking him down, and then standing him up, and cutting him dreadfully, he begging for his life. His wife, having fainted away, was lying on the floor.

This went on until day began to dawn, when they left, cursing and threatening to burn his house over his head. The cord was unloosened from the neck of Mr. Albertson, and the deep gashes dressed. He received severe injury, and will bear the scars thereof through life, for I am thankful to say his life is not despaired of. Great indignation prevails, and a plan has been devised by the people to protect themselves from such great evil in future. A company of young men is to be associated, to ride about on horseback all night; twelve to go out at once, and are relieved at a certain hour by others. They are well armed, and will give the alarm where they discover signs of an intended attack. Richard Thompson is their leader, a bold, intrepid man.

Wednesday, October, 1780

Last night Mr. Burr, a storekeeper, was asleep in the store (as was his custom, for the purpose of guarding it), when he was aroused by a noise at the window, which was so heavily barred that though they bored the shutter, and tugged at it a great while, they could not open it. Near the top of the shutter there is unfortunately a small opening to admit the light. Through this one of the villains put his gun and fired, killing Mr. Burr. The ball passed through his body, as he was sitting up in bed. The wretches then fled, and their victim lived but a few moments, just long enough to tell the particulars.

When will deliverance come?

3
THE HESSIANS

THE BRITISH HIRED GERMAN TROOPS to fight for them in the colonies. As many of these paid soldiers were from the Germanic state of Hesse-Kassel, they were called Hessians. About 30,000 Hessians fought in the war. Each Hessian received about twenty-five cents a day as his pay.

Like most Americans, Mary despised the Hessians, mainly because they were forced to let these foreigners live in their homes. The soldiers irritated them by getting drunk on payday, carousing, eating the family's food, and using up the household supply of stove wood.

Out of the original large group of Hessian soldiers sent to America to fight, forty percent died in battle or of disease, or deserted the army to stay in America. In fact, both Benjamin Franklin and George Washington came up with plans to entice the Hessians to desert. In one clever plan, leaflets were printed in German and wrapped around plugs of chewing tobacco. They were then tossed where the Hessians would be sure to find them.

As the war dragged on, more and more Hessians

deserted the British army for several reasons. First, they were not particularly interested in the British cause—after all it was not the Hessians' war. Secondly, they saw the potential America offered, mainly the large amounts of low-cost land. And finally, most Hessians had little to look forward to in Germany if they went back. So thousands did not go back, instead they sent for their wives and children to join them in the new land.

Early in the war, a now famous attack and American victory over the Hessians took place. On Christmas night 1776, General Washington's men took every boat they could find and crossed the Delaware River in the freezing rain and surprised the Hessian troops at Trenton, New Jersey. The entire crossing took nine hours and Washington's tattered troops had to withstand dreadful cold, ice floes in the river, hunger, and the difficulty of keeping their gunpowder dry. The Hessians were warm and dry

The flight of the Hessians after the battle at Trenton, December 26, 1776

This drawing of a Hessian soldier suggests the attitudes of the colonists toward the mercenaries.

and had spent Christmas day and evening celebrating. They were off guard and asleep when the Americans attacked in the early morning hours of Thursday, December 26, 1776.

Taken by surprise, nearly 1,000 Hessians gave up and were taken prisoner. The Americans also took stores of food, guns, and powder. This victory and another one at Princeton a few days later on January 3, 1777, gave the Americans new courage. But with only 4,000 men in his army, Washington was unable to hold either Trenton or Princeton and he took his troops into the hills around Morristown, New Jersey, to spend the winter.

As the fighting of 1776 came to an end, the Americans knew that they had won two minor victories, knew that the British were no closer to decisive victory than they were before, and knew that hope was rising that Americans might yet win this war.

The improved military position didn't help Mary and her neighbors, however, and they remained deeply distressed by the presence of enemy troops. Housing soldiers with local civilians is called quartering and it was a common practice in Europe and America at the time.

Quartering troops in civilian homes was such a hated practice that it was prohibited by the Third Amendment to the Constitution. Even before the Constitution and Bill of Rights were created, Americans had put in writing their hatred of foreign mercenaries. In the Declaration of Independence Americans expressed their belief in their right to govern themselves, and told the world specifically why the king of England was unfit to rule the American colonists. Included in this long list of grievances against King George are the following charges:

> He [George III] has kept among us, in times of peace, Standing Armies without the Consent of our legislatures.

> For quartering large bodies of armed troops among us:

> He is at this time transporting large Armies of foreign Mercenaries to complete the works of death, desolation and tyranny, already begun with circumstances of Cruelty & perfidy scarcely paralleled in the most barbarous ages, and totally unworthy [of] the Head of a civilized nation.

Tuesday, October 16, 1776

RATION DAY. The Hessians borrowed a young horse of Mr. Pattison, to fetch home their rations, taking a pail for the liquor. After two hours' absence they drove up, cursing with rage at the horse, and whipping the poor creature most unmercifully. The reason was soon manifest. It seems, just as one of them had set a pail of spirits in the wagon, the young horse reared on his hind legs, and upset the whole!

We could scarcely conceal our pleasure on hearing this, well knowing we had escaped one horrible jollification at all events, thanks to the high-mettled animal.

44

Thursday

Once a month the Hessians go to headquarters for their rations, including spirits, and then for three days they are for the most part given up to intoxication, and we have trying and grievous scenes to go through; fighting, brawls, drumming and fifing, and dancing the night long; card and dice playing, and every abomination going on under our very roofs! The noise from the kitchen, which they always occupy, is terrifying. The door opening into the rest of the house is nailed fast, but the inmates are continually in dread of having their dwellings burnt over their heads.

Tuesday, October

The Hessians have been ordered to cut down all the saplings they can find. They pile them along the road about twelve feet high, then pressing teams and wagons, they cart it away to forts and barracks at a distance.

It is a serious loss; in a few years our farms will be without wood for use. They (the Hessians) burn an immense quantity;—even the rail fences, unless we take care to cut the cart wood for their constant use. Keeping the fire a-going all night, many a poor farmer rises in the morning to find his cattle strayed miles away, or his grain trampled down and ruined!

The practice of "pressing" (from "impressing") also angered the Long Islanders. Pressing meant that the British soldiers forcibly took items or animals they wanted, claiming they were required for the war. Presses were used to get food, wood, horses, and even soldiers and sailors if needed. The Americans hated pressing and tried every way possible to prevent the English soldiers from getting what they wanted. Their efforts were rarely successful as the British stopped at nothing in their efforts to find and seize necessary supplies.

Monday, December, 1776

Henry Pattison, the nearest neighbor, has eight sturdy sons, and one little timid daughter. He belongs to the Society of Friends, is a fine specimen of humanity, owns a valuable farm, yet has a pretty hard struggle to bring up his large family. He was beginning to prosper a little, when the war began; but he is a mild, patient, pious man, consulted in all troubles and difficulties the whole country round; has prevented much going to law; visits the sick in soul and body, and relieves them by his judicious advice, temporal and spiritual. He is called hereabouts The Peace-Maker.

Friend Pattison appears to have neither "part nor lot" in the struggle in which the country is engaged. How strange! *To be a man, and remain neutral!* His soul abhors War. The principle of their sect is enrooted in his breast. Yet he is a severe sufferer from it. Six Hessians are quartered upon him. They took possession of the kitchen; swung up their hammocks; cook his (the farmer's) food, and hang about, smoking and drinking the live-long day. Dear, how annoying! When shall we be rid of them?

In her next entry Mary admits to another fear concerning the Hessians: that her children, especially Charles, are growing too fond of these foreign enemy soldiers.

Early January, 1777

The soldiers take so much notice of the children, that I fear lest they should contract evil, especially Charles. They have taught him to speak their language; he understands nearly all their conversation. They make pretty willow baskets for Marcia and Grace, and tell them of their own little ones at home, over the stormy ocean. The children are fond of them, and they feel no enmity toward them. What is more melancholy than the trade of a hired soldier? I deeply commiserate their wretched lot. Nothing to ennoble the contest; no homes and hearths to fight for; no country to save; no freedom to bleed and die for. It may be "sweet and proper for our country to die," as saith the old Roman, but it is bitter servitude to risk life and limb for lucre; and revolting, sickening, to serve in a cause by which we have nothing to gain in victory, or to lose in defeat!

Later in the same month Mary's attention shifts from her hatred of the Hessians to the joyful news of the colonial victory at Princeton, New Jersey, a victory that electrified the countryside.

She is saddened, however, by the death of General Hugh Mercer, a valiant soldier and physician. As General Mercer was leading his colonial troops toward Princeton, he was attacked by two British regiments. Mercer's riflemen were forced to retreat. An early shot hit General Mercer's horse, knocking the general to the ground. British soldiers, believing that Mercer was General Washington, smashed Mercer's head with the butt of a musket. He was then stabbed seven times in the body and twice in the head.

Washington, seeing Mercer's troops retreating, galloped to the head of the troops and stopped the panicked soldiers by shouting to them to hold their ground. Riding a white horse he marched the colonial soldiers toward the British line. The colonials fired and the British began dropping back. When the smoke had cleared, Washington sat unharmed on his white horse.

With this victory the British were driven out of western New Jersey and Americans everywhere began to feel that they might indeed win this war!

January 15, 1777

News of the Battle of Princeton. My husband safe, thank Heaven! General Washington victorious; General Mercer mortally wounded! How the thoughts of his loved ones rush to my heart! God have mercy on them! The Commander-in-Chief, by his judgment, skill, and

An early engraving of Washington's victory at Princeton carries this description: "At this important crisis, the soul of Washington rose superior to danger, seizing a standard he advanced uncovered before the Column and reining his steed towards the enemy with his sword flashing in the rays of the rising sun, he waved on the troops behind him to the charge. Insprited by his example the Militia sprang forward and delivered an effective fire which stopped the progress of the enemy."

cool intrepidity, has struck the enemy with surprise. They have looked with contempt on our raw men, many of whom never saw a battle. They expected to crush us; to quell with ease, by their giant power, the

48

rebels, as the lord of the forest crushes the insects beneath his feet.

They forget the deep-rooted indignation which burns in our breasts; the determination to be free, animating the whole colonies with one heart and purpose, to do and dare for liberty, or death!

Only once in *Personal Recollections* does Mary say anything good about the Hessians. She admits that when they are around, robbers and looters stay away.

Monday, January, 1778

There is an old proverb which saith, "It is an ill wind which blows nobody good." The Hessians and soldiers billeted about here for six months past, left today for the mainland campaign, and the robbery, from which we have for some time been exempt, will now go on again. The villains feared the soldiery; dreadful tax as it is to keep *them*, it is nothing in comparison to the other evil.

On Thursday of the same week she tells how her fears have come true and that she thinks the robbers are far worse than the Hessians.

The robbers have been over already; they landed last night at the harbor. In the dead of night they surrounded the house of John Pearsall. He is called rich, and there is no doubt they counted on large booty. Their first care is generally to prevent escapes, lest the alarm should be given to the neighbors. Whenever they have reason to think that anyone has escaped to inform, they invariably scamper, fearing surprise. On finding his house so hemmed in, Mr. Pearsall, who was the only man in the house, made a great noise and blustering, called Tom, John, and Harry to load and fire, then ran to the top of the house with a gun, and fired three times in quick succession. The robbers took the alarm, jumped into the boat, and shoved off. They were fired upon, but I know not whether injured, but trust not, for they surely are not fit to die.

Much later she writes:

Monday, October, 1780

This neighborhood is still infested with the odious Hessians. They are so filthy and lazy, lounging about all day long, smoking and sleeping. The patience of the good Friends is inexhaustible. After filling up their parlors, kitchens, and bedrooms, the whole winter with chests, liquor-casks, hammocks, birdcages, guns, boots, and powder flasks, they were last week ordered to Jamaica [New York]. Oh the rejoicing! It *would* flash out of the eye, though the Friends' discreet tongues spake it not.

The moment the Hessians took their leave Friend Pattison caused the broken places in the wall to be repaired, for the Colonel's lady had the room ornamented all around with stuffed parrots, perched on sticks driven in the wall. The quarterly meeting of the Society is near at hand. They expect friends and relations to stop with them, and make preparations for their reception.

Well, all were putting their houses in order, when the appalling news spread like wildfire—*"The Hessians are coming back!"*

Running to the window, I descried them in the distance like a cloud of locusts, dusky and dim; but the fife and drum, assailing our ears, if we needed additional evidence, convinced us that it was too true. They had indeed been ordered back. How many tears of vexation I shed!

Thursday, October, 1780

The neighborhood has been more quiet for a week past, and Hessians have really left, bag and baggage, for which Heaven be praised! They are like the locusts of Egypt, desolating the land, and eating up every green thing.

After this entry, *Personal Recollections* does not reveal any other information about the Hessians, good or bad, until the war ends. Then, with victory assured, Mary seems to take some pity on the Hessians who have to go back to Germany and writes that those Hessians who decide to stay in America choose to do so because the colonists treated them better than they had any right to expect. She still does not think they are in the same social class as she and her friends.

April 23, 1783

The soldiers and Hessians are moving off in bands, and the sick are left behind to follow after. Many of the poor creatures have formed attachments, and the ties of kindness and gratitude are hard to break. The human heart, of whatever clime or station, will respond to good treatment; and it is cheering and delightful to observe that, in spite of the greatest personal inconvenience, by patience and good offices, we may awaken interest and gratitude in those beneath us.

4

REVOLUTIONARY HEROES

MANY OF MARY'S JOURNAL ENTRIES mention people who were to be heroes in the Revolutionary War. A few, such as Nathan Hale and George Washington, became famous Americans and appear in histories of the period. Others, like Mary's son, Charles, are ordinary people whose heroic acts show the determination of the American patriots.

Personal Recollections tells first of Nathan Hale. Washington wanted to send out spies to discover where Lord Sir Howe might next strike the rebel army. Nathan Hale of Connecticut, a twenty-four-year-old schoolteacher, volunteered to be a spy. Hale was a captain in a ranger company, and was also a poet, an expert checker player, and a powerful kicker in a game similar to soccer.

Mary describes Hale's mission and its unfortunate end. Nathan Hale had almost completed his drawings of British troop locations when he was caught and arrested. The British found the drawings in his shoes. He confessed and was hanged without a trial. Before the noose was put around his neck, Hale wrote to his mother and a fellow officer. Afterwards, those who had witnessed his execution praised Hale as a man who met his death bravely as a hero.

October 3 1776

Dear, dear husband! was there ever anything so sorrowful, so dreadful, as young Nathan Hale's fate? Tears are running down while I write.

Would that the enemy's designs could have been discovered without so costly a sacrifice! Gen. Washington desired, for he knew it to be of vital importance to the Continental Forces, that someone should penetrate the British Camp, to discover their plan.

In the performance of this duty, the flower of the army has fallen a victim to British wrath and brutality.

Rhoda Pemberton wrote me that at the time when Colonel Knowlton first made known to the officers the wish of the Commander-in-Chief [to send out a spy], a dead silence prevailed; and then Captain Hale looked up and said, "I will undertake it." It seemed, she said, against right and nature to all his friends, and even to strangers, that so young and gallant an officer should go out on such service. But young Hale said, "Every kind of service for his country became honorable. It was desired by the Commander of her armies."

Young Captain Hale left the camp at Harlem Heights under General Washington's orders, late in last month, I believe.

Before reaching the British lines he assumed the dress of a school master; he wore a suit of brown broadcloth, and a round broad-brimmed hat.

He took off his silver shoe buckles too. His college diploma was in his port-manteau, signed by the Revered Doctor Napthali Daggett of Yale University.

He passed, so Rhoda tells me, safely through the British lines, everywhere, along the posts, and among the tents and barracks, to Huntington, about nine miles from this place. It was the place from which he

Nathan Hale, in disguise, enters the camp of the enemy.

started a short time before. A boat was to meet him, to sail over to Connecticut Main.

The young man went down to the shore at daybreak in perfect security; no doubt buoyed with joy at the success of his enterprise.

He saw a boat moving shoreward. *It was the enemy!* He did retreat, but around the neck, out of sight. Thither the young man was taken, and put in irons.

His papers, written in some dead language (Latin, I believe), were under the soles of his pumps. They betrayed him.

The next morning at daybreak, after he received sentence, he was executed.

"I only regret," he said, just before he ascended to

The execution of Nathan Hale

the gibbet, "that I have but one life to lose for my country."

Rhoda gave me this account. She says that Prevost Cunningham (the inhuman wretch!) called out, "Swing the Rebel off!"

I cannot write this without weeping. It was a noble testimony, but a bitter necessity. So likely, so young, so brave.

It was on the 21st of September '76. They [The British] tore up the letter he wrote to his family, saying the rebels should never know they had a man in their army who could die with such firmness.

Mary noted that Nathan Hale was seized by British soldiers only nine miles from her father's parsonage. In her next letter to her husband she tells of her delight in the heroism shown by a hero right under her own roof. Her young son Charles's actions saved the family horse from being taken by the British. Mary knows that not all heroes are written about in history books and she wants her husband to be proud of his teenage revolutionary son.

Tuesday, December, 1776

A press for horses yesterday. I will relate how Charley saved our young horse. He and James Pattison were idly sitting on the fence, the other side of the pond, talking indignantly of the insults of the British, to whom Charley shows no mercy, when they espied a light-horseman at the door of a farmhouse. They knew the [soldiers'] next place would be Isaac Willetts', which, though only across the pond, is completely hid from our view by a stately row of poplars, which form a leafy screen; and they knew his errand too, that he would be here in an instant, for when "pressing," they gallop from house to house with violent speed.

"Fleetfoot shall not go," said Charles, "without an effort to save him," and running with all his might to the barn he jumped on [the horse's] back, and made for the woods.

On the instant he was seen by the redcoat, who put spurs to his horse, and came on a full run toward the woods, where Charles had disappeared. My heart beat quick when the redcoat too was lost to sight. My dear, brave child might fall from his horse and be dashed against the trees, in the hot pursuit of the light-horseman.

My father and I sat gazing intently toward the woods, awaiting the result in breathless anxiety, astonished at the boy's daring, and ready to reprove his rash spirit in attempting to save the young horse at the risk of his own safety.

In about an hour's time we saw the redcoat come out of the woods below; he stopped a man in the road

The Politician, *a satirical drawing by William Hogarth*

and made inquiries, but getting no satisfaction, rode off, muttering curses.

At nightfall, peeping his way through the wood, Charles made his appearance, still mounted on his favorite Fleetfoot. By signs we made known to him that the danger had passed, and he rode up to the house. Overjoyed to see him, he told us his story, which Grace and Marcia drank in with greedy ears. Indeed the scene in the porch was worthy of Hogarth's pencil. [William Hogarth (1697–1764) was a British painter, engraver, and printmaker whose satirical illus-

trations were popular in England and the colonies.]
On one side was his pale affrighted mother, and the little girls, with eyes open wide and full of wonder; near by, the venerable grandfather, with silver locks parted upon a peaceful brow, and Charley standing close to his steed, as he recounted his wrongs and hairbreadth escape, leaning his head occasionally against his proud neck, so that my son's curls of gold mingled with the mane of Fleetfoot.

He said that he struck deeper and deeper into the woods, going from one piece to another, until the forest became very dense and dark. He rode into a tangled, marshy place, where he stood five hours without moving!

At one time he heard his pursuer close by, heard his fearful oaths, heard him lashing the sides of his own jaded horse. Charley's heart beat violently. But the bog was wet and gloomy, and the soldier's ardor was dampened—he durst not venture. So Charles and Fleetfoot were left to themselves in the deep wood. A brave feat for a boy of fourteen!

George Washington played an important part in winning the war. He was a good general who kept the American army together even though he didn't have enough horses, weapons, ammunition, food, uniforms, or money to pay his soldiers. Congress sent him as much as possible, but it was not enough and usually arrived too late.

The Continental Congress made a wise choice when it asked Washington to take command of its armies and give citizen farmers some military training. Under the military rules in place at the time, Revolutionary War soldiers joined the army for a few months and then went home (if they chose to) when their time was up. Sometimes the soldiers were paid for their service and sometimes they were not. On more than one occasion George Washington promised to pay the men with his own money if they would just stay with him a little longer. He also asked rich merchants, such

*George Washington taking command of the Army
at Cambridge, Massachusetts, 1775*

as Robert Morris, to lend cash to pay the troops and spies. After Washington's victories over the British at Trenton and Princeton, though, Congress took steps to extend the period of enlistment and to give the men better training and pay.

Through the war years, General Washington lost more battles than he won. However, his troops were fighting against a larger and better-trained enemy. The actual tally at the end of the war was three battles won, nine lost, and one tie. And in spite of this battle record, historians agree that Washington was an extraordinary leader who carried the army and the American nation to victory. Part of the reason for his greatness was his determination, his

59

courage, and his devotion to the cause of liberty. He remains a hero to all Americans.

Friday, January, 1777

General Washington has completely dislodged the British along the Delaware river, and recovered almost the whole province of New Jersey. Does it not teach a man to look to Him, and remember who it is that blesses the means, when to mortal view they seem totally inadequate?

Tuesday, August, 1777

Congress has passed important resolutions, and increased General Washington's power, investing him with unlimited command. They are endeavoring to rouse the people by an impressive Address. Benjamin Franklin, Silas Deane, and Arthur Lee, are sent to solicit aid of foreign powers.

Personal Recollections next describes the American army's brilliant victory over the British at Saratoga, New York. This victory is recognized as the turning point of the war. Because of it, France and Spain were willing to help the rebels, and both of these countries initiated efforts to send soldiers, supplies, and warships to the colonies.

The Battle of Saratoga showed the world that the Continental army had at least a fifty-fifty chance of winning the war. The American strategy was to prevent Britain from dividing the colonies and thus being able to conquer them one by one.

France had been planning for some time to aid the colonies and gain revenge on its old enemy, England. But after the British General John Burgoyne surrendered his troops to a colonial force at Saratoga, French leaders believed that England might be willing to begin peace talks with the colonials. France feared an early end to the war, as this would allow Britain to quickly recover and rebuild its army, and be strong again. The French invited an American delegation to a conference during February of 1778. At this conference an alliance was worked out in which the French and the Americans pledged friendship and cooperation. Included was a promise from France to aid America through trade and direct financial assistance. In June of 1778, France formally entered the war as an ally of the colonies. Spain waited a year and then joined the war as an ally of France.

Lydia writes:

Heaven be praised! We have just heard of your safety, and of *the surrender*, though it happened so long since.

General Arnold has gained a bright laurel in the affair; he proved himself a skilful and brave officer. The surrender excites great astonishment among the British hereabouts. "Discretion is the better part of valor," thought Burgoyne, his troops worn out, and his situation becoming more and more critical. Your letters, stained and yellow, looked indeed as though they had come from the wars. I suppose we receive only about one in six.

The American cause seems to assume a brighter aspect since this event [the victory at Saratoga]. It will doubtless inspire confidence in its ultimate success. The cause of freedom—Heaven grant it!

Other entries in the journal note how much the Americans are helped in their war effort by the French and other Europeans.

September 10, 1780
The battle of Camden. 16th August. Hard fought. The Continentals defeated. Baron de Kalb, a Prussian gentleman, slain. The second officer in command.

The greater part of our forces, militia, who fled at the first fire, and could not be rallied, which I cannot find in my woman's heart to condemn, dear as freedom is to its every pulse. I can so vividly fancy myself standing up for the first time before the enemy's murderous batteries, and the courage oozing out at my finger ends.

Tuesday

News today of the arrival of another French fleet. Seven ships of the line; 6,000 land troops, commanded by Count de Rochambeau, at Rhode Island.

[This news] Will give new life to Congress and the army.

October 5th

A letter from my husband; still inactive, the South having now become the principal seat of action, which I do not regret. The French fleet returned to France! Thus has perished our hope of naval assistance. It seems unaccountable. The land forces remain.

Personal Recollections next tells of the famous American, Major General Benedict Arnold, hero of Ticonderoga and Saratoga and also one of America's most infamous traitors. How did this treachery occur?

The Americans were cheered by the arrival of French ships at Rhode Island in 1780.

Benedict Arnold became a very bitter man after the Battle of Saratoga. He had been passed over for promotion in 1777 and wanted to leave the army. However, George Washington talked him into staying. In October of 1777 Arnold fought bravely and was wounded in the Second Battle of Freeman's Farm. His superior, General Gates, won credit for the victory. In 1778 Arnold took command of Philadelphia where he met and married a young society woman, Margaret Shippen. They lived an extravagant lifestyle and he was actually accused of being a Tory sympathizer. He was brought up to a court-martial but cleared of these charges. Arnold brooded over what he considered to be poor treatment from his country and he began to correspond with the enemy. In 1780, when he was in command of West Point, Arnold worked out a plan to surrender the fort to the British general, Sir Henry Clinton. Before the plan could be carried out, the Americans captured British Major John André, who was carrying papers sent by Arnold to the British. Major André was hanged, but Arnold escaped capture and sailed for England and safety. Mary's letters and journal entries show how much Arnold's betrayal shocked her, as it did most Americans. She was disgusted by his treachery.

Arnold never achieved much happiness or success in England. The British government gave him land in Canada, but he had little use for it. He spent most of the rest of his life as a merchant in the West Indies. In the end, he was burdened with debt, heartsick, and not trusted even by his British friends.

Thursday

A deeply interesting document from Edward, in which is recorded a most detestable and flagrant instance of treachery.

The Lord be praised, we have been delivered from the consequences!

A plot of General Benedict Arnold for giving into the hands of the enemy the fortress of West Point! Who

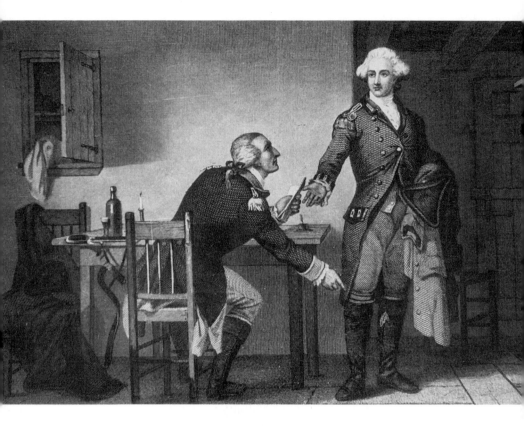

An artist's representation of the Treason of Benedict Arnold *shows the bitter Arnold (seated) instructing Major André to conceal messages to the British in his boot.*

can imagine what might have been the result had not the despicable design been providentially frustrated?

Arnold has acted with bravery in several actions. It is said the cause of his dreadful defection is that the laurels which he won at Saratoga were awarded to General Gates by Congress, and but little notice taken of his valor on that occasion. Is this any excuse for such Satanic revenge? A bad man, and never a true lover of his country.

A patriot would drain his heart's blood for her, even though she should prove ungrateful.

Saturday

General Greene appointed to the command of the Southern division.

Friday, October, 1780

Public affairs engage but little attention hereabouts; each family is absorbed in its own toils and privations.

Benedict Arnold has received, as a reward of treachery, the appointment of Brigadier-General in the British army, and it is said, a large amount of money besides. Small compensation for the forfeiture of honor, principle, reputation, *all* that man holds dear! A bold, ambitious, bad man, pitiless and selfish, he betrayed his country from the unworthy motive of revenge. True, he served her nobly in the expedition to Quebec, and proved himself on other occasions a fearless officer, and Congress awarded too little praise, and acted perhaps unwisely in promoting younger men before him; but personal aggrandizement, and not patriotism, actuated him; while the love of freedom, devotion to right and justice, is the principle of action of Washington, Greene, and Montgomery, whose memory many a tear will embalm, and whose heroic bravery, beauty, graceful attractiveness, and melancholy fate, will form the theme of praise and regret to beings yet unborn.

NIGHTS
OF TEARS

PERSONAL RECOLLECTIONS describes the way Mary's family and neighbors were forced to live during the seven years of the British occupation of Long Island. It gives us a clear picture of how difficult life can become for ordinary people with an enemy army camped on the doorstep. Not all the suffering and loss in wartime occur on the battlefield.

Between 1776 and 1778, Mary and her family lived, as did many other people in the northeastern colonies, in almost daily fear for their lives. The shock of the British landing in the waters of New York with 32,000 disciplined soldiers, and the retreat of the American army after sustaining more than 1,000 casualties terrified the Islanders. Not only were the British to be feared; law and order broke down. Long Island was to endure continual strife, conflict, and bloodshed until December 4, 1783, the day that the last British troops left the area.

The British did not try very hard to stop the robbing, looting, and wanton destruction on the Island by bands of robbers, kidnappers, and thugs; peaceful, ordinary citizens had to protect themselves as best they could. Sometimes they had the will and the weapons to do so, and sometimes they had neither and were not able to defend themselves. Mary writes of a woman with four small children who barely escaped the wrath of a British officer, and describes the brutal slaying of her good friend's husband, Nathaniel Woodhull. But though she weeps for her friend, she feels great pride in the cause for which her friend's husband gave his life. Mary and her neighbors are continually frustrated by their inability to stop the violent acts that became part of everyday life under an enemy flag.

Friday, October, 1776
Morning

The Pattisons had a fine young heifer killed during the night. Some of the family heard the noise, but thought it most prudent not to make any resistance. The creature was drawn and quartered in the barn. What boldness!

Mrs. Clement, the wife of James Clement, was alone in the house with her children yesterday, about two miles hence, when an officer rode up, dismounted, and entered. He told her very civilly that he wanted supper for his company (about sixty men). She politely declined. He then began to insist, and at length said they *should* come. Mrs. Clement replied that it was out of the question. She had nothing prepared; no person to assist her, and four little children to take care of. Still he rode off, saying they would be back in an hour for supper, and if she did not get it ready, she must take the consequences.

She sat in fear and trembling through the hour, and her helplessness overcame her so that she could not resist tears most of the time, though she tried to put her trust in the Lord, that He would deliver her from her distress.

She thought it would be well if she could take her

children and leave the house, but the nearest neighbor was a mile by the road, though only half that distance through the woods. But the wood was often infested with robbers, and the very thought of going that way made her shudder. In her state of weakness and fear she was quite unable to carry her baby, and the three little ones were unable to walk the distance of a mile. So she determined to wait the event, and when the British came to tell them the truth.

Whether they found a better prospect elsewhere, or what the seeming cause was, I cannot say; but they did not return, and I cannot help believing that they were providentially deterred from so doing.

In the next letter, Mary tells Edward about the shocking murder of her dear friend's husband. Her friend Ruth Woodhull was a member of one of Long Island's most illustrious families—the Floyds. Ruth's brother, William Floyd, was a renowned country squire and one of four New Yorkers to sign the Declaration of Independence. He was a major general in the militia, a representative to the First Continental Congress, and a state senator. He and his brother-in-law, General Nathaniel Woodhull (Ruth Floyd's husband), led the patriots in their neighborhood of Long Island. Throughout the Revolutionary War and well into the 1800s, the Floyd family helped America to industrialize. The Floyd estate at Mastic, Long Island, still exists and is now a museum.

Saturday, October, 1776

Ruth Floyd's husband (you remember Ruth, my old friend) has been murdered!

She married Nathaniel Woodhull. He was elected last year President of the Provincial Congress. There are no bounds to the indignation and horror. A pattern of Christian meekness must he or she be, to be able to forgive and pray for such enemies. But that God will turn their hearts I do most fervently implore.

I jot down a few of the particulars, although it is a painful task.

His duty was to drive the livestock from the shore to the interior of the island, out of reach of the enemy.

Being poorly off for men, he was forced to wait for a reinforcement at Jamaica. He was Brigadier-General of Suffolk and Queens.

The General fell a victim of his high sense of honor. He refused to abandon his perilous post while any hope of reinforcement remained.

My father thinks that he would have been justified in withdrawal. His force was reduced to less than 100 men, from a desire to remove their families to places of safety. [The men left service to go home and take their families to safety.]

Those remaining were worn down, and their horses over-driven, in repelling the ravaging parties of the enemy. The British (landing at Gravesend) were pouring over the Island in swarms, cutting off communications with the American force at Brooklyn.

A severe thunderstorm compelled him to take refuge in an inn near by. He was overtaken by the 17th regiment of British Dragoons. The General gave up his sword in token of surrender.

A ruffian ordered him to say, "God save the King." The General replied, "God save us all," on which the cowardly assassin brutally assaulted the defenseless General with a broad sword.

He would have killed him, but his hand was arrested by an officer of more magnanimity and honor.

One arm was horribly mangled, from shoulder to hand. In this situation he was dragged from place to place. At length he was released from a filthy little vessel used to transport livestock for the use of the British army by the enemy, and removed, mangled, bleeding, and parched with fever heat, to an inn at Jamaica, Mrs. Hinchman's tavern.

She gave up the best room and bed for the poor

The capture of General Woodhull
outside an inn, August 1776

wounded General's use. He begged her not to leave him alone in the hands of the enemy. The humane woman answered, "Don't be uneasy, General; I don't expect to go to bed tonight."

The next day he was taken westward again. Mrs. Hinchman had dressed the wounds, bandaged his head, which was terribly cut, and the shattered arm.

At a half-way house, while the escort regaled themselves within, the wounded General was left with a guard, under the horse-shed! Here again a woman acted the part of the good Samaritan. Mrs. Howard, the landlady, went out to minister to the weak and fainting patriot.

She brought bread, and wine-sangaree, [a mixture of wine and lemonade] and invited him with tender pity and solicitude, to partake of some refreshment.

The guard impudently asked, "If she had nothing for them?"

"I *give* to prisoners, you can *buy*," the kind woman replied.

The fainting General was conveyed to New Utrecht. He felt himself rapidly growing worse; his little remaining strength was fast ebbing. He urgently requested that his wife might be sent for. Strange to say, the request was granted. The arm was cut off by the surgeon, but mortification [gangrene] took place, and the brave man breathed his last, his wife, Ruth, having arrived only in time to receive his dying sign.

Poor Ruth! What must have been her feelings when the news of her husband's state reached Mastick!

Rhoda [Rhoda Pemberton] writes that she was wonderfully sustained, and showed great presence of mind. She (Ruth Woodhull) had caused a wagon-load of provisions to be put up; but little could her poor husband partake of.

General Woodhull lived but a few hours after she reached New Utrecht. He was in the enemy hospital, in a comfortless, wretched condition. It was his request that Ruth should distribute the provisions among the poor starved American prisoners there, which she did, and then placed her dear, lost husband's body in the wagon, and went on her lonely way home.

Poor woman.

Yet as she travelled that dreary journey of 70 miles,

there must have been some comfort in the thought that the precious remains of her gallant husband were not left with the enemy, to be denied the rites of sepulture [burial]; but that she could lay him by the side of his forefathers, in the family burial place; in hope, and honorable pride, that for his country he had laid down his life.

Although Mary and her family have a hard life during the occupation, they seem to have been spared a lot of the suffering their neighbors had to endure at the hands of robbers and bandits. For their good fortune, she knows she must be thankful that there are British soldiers quartered in the house. While they are present, the thieves and murderers stay away. She admits that it makes her feel strange to feel gratitude to an enemy.

Mary stays awake nights thinking about the horrors going on all around her, not all of which were an enemy dealing with another enemy in a battle. She and her neighbors, for instance, were unwilling observers of British military discipline and the incident so unnerved Mary that she endured nightmares for months.

Monday, November, 1777

On every Monday exercising is practiced opposite our house. Today, when the maneuvering was over, a man who had been found intoxicated the night before was stripped and whipped severely, with a rattan, till the blood streamed down his back. Oh, it is dreadful to witness such horrors! I fled from the sight, but the heart-piercing cries of the poor creature followed me. I could no longer refrain from running out of the house, and begging them to desist. They paid no attention, and closed the gate upon me. The rattan struck his cheek, perhaps by accident, cut it open, and it bled terribly! I screamed out "MURDER!" They were startled, and stopped. The appealing look of gratitude I received from the poor maimed soldier was sweet reward.

Mary Pattison, whose sympathy for the suffering never failed, took the poor creature in; commiserating his pitiful condition, she dressed his wounds, which were frightfully deep, and like the good Samaritan, poured in the oil of consolation.

Mary worries constantly about her husband, wondering if he has been killed and if she is now a widow. She writes:

Friday, November, 1777

Days of agony and nights of tears are my experience; the agony of suspense, the tears of widowhood! In imagination I have no longer a husband! He is slain on the field of battle, of which no tidings have come; or the victim of neglected wounds and disease, he is in the hands of the enemy. If alive and at liberty, we surely should long ago have heard from him. How can I endure it? Oh, God, endue me with patience, or I sink! Thy protection is for those who trust in thee. Do I? Oh, Lord, help me, I pray thee!

Mary continues to write in her journal of the things that are happening all around. She laments that even young children are victims during a war. She tells of a neighbor being shot in a robbery. Another neighbor is killed by thugs searching his house for gold. She wonders if peace and order will ever be restored to her homeland.

Monday, January, 1777

Were I to undertake to relate the injuries, insults, horrors, and sufferings our poor farmers are subject to, I should never finish the story. They take the fence rails to burn, so that the fields are all left open, and the cattle stray away and are often lost; burn fires all night on the ground, and to replenish them, go to the woods and cut down all the young saplings, thereby destroying the growth of ages. But worse than all, robbers come over from the main shore in boats, and keep us in constant alarm! They belong to no party, and spare none; freebooters, cowardly midnight assassins, incendiaries, bold, and daring. "Their hand is against every man, and every man's hand is against them."

We have been spared as yet on account of the Hessians and officer, which are quartered here, whom they fear. Thus "some strange comfort every state attends."

Monday, March, 1777

James Parker, a farmer near by, was driving home late last evening, from the town; the night was uncommonly dark. He passed a large tree; behind it stood a man with a loaded gun. A voice called out to the traveller to stop; it was unheeded. The robber fired and hit him; he fell off his seat and expired!

The horses took fright, and running three miles, came to a noted tavern kept by Increase Carpenter, where they stopped under a shed, and stood still until morning, when they were discovered with their sad burden, the dead man! The goods in the wagon were of course untouched, owing to the horses running away. The indignation of the people is without bounds, and very active measures of defense are talked of.

Thursday, January, 1778

A band of ruffians entered the house of Mr. Miller at East Hampton, at midnight, when the men folk were absent. Mrs. Miller caught up her youngest child, an infant, and ran out at the back door; the next, a little boy of four years, crept under a table to get out of sight. But one of the creatures spied him, and saying, "Here's a d____d little rebel," stuck his poignard [dagger] into his thigh, making a severe wound. Think of the savage hardness of the heart of the man, who would inflict injury upon an innocent helpless child!

Saturday evening, January, 1778

A tale of horror has just come to our ears; we have not heard the details, nor do I wish to, they are so horrible. It seems the Runners entered the house of John Wilson and threatened [him], until the wife, to save the life of her husband, revealed [their] hiding-place. But it was too late; he died the next morning from a sabre cut which he then received, cleaving the skull and occasioning so great a loss of blood. The villains took a large sum of money, which was in silver coin, in bags under the hearthstone. Mr. Wilson was much beloved in the neighborhood; his death produced the greatest excitement and indignation.

I went over to Henry Pattison's this evening. He, with his wife, had just returned from the scene of the dreadful catastrophe; they had never witnessed anything more distressing than Mrs. Wilson's state—wringing her hands continually with grief and horror, and at times quite out of her mind. A great company is out in search of the robbers.

Monday, January, 1778

Two of the three were taken last evening, the other had gone off with the money. It is said that the serving girl connived with the thieves, one of whom was her cousin. How awful to contemplate! I suppose Tory influence will screen [protect] them; they were sent to New York this morning strongly guarded. The times are so disordered, that we have to keep still, and bear everything; complaint seemeth utterly useless.

6
LOVE
AND
FRIENDSHIP

HOUSING WAS AN ENORMOUS PROBLEM for both enemy and patriot during the American Revolution. British generals built some army camps with tents for the men to live in; however, they seldom had enough camps or tents. The solution was to put men in the homes of colonial civilians—friendly ones if possible; and in rebel homes if necessary. The word for this practice was *quartering*. A group of Hessian soldiers and a wounded British major and his aide were assigned to the parsonage during the occupation of Long Island. The officer, Major Charles Musgrave, had been seriously wounded by a bullet and suffered grievously from his wound which did not seem to heal. Mary shouldered much of the responsibility for his care in addition to her household chores and her duties to her family.

Caring for the sick and wounded is never an easy task, but it was much harder in the eighteenth century than it is today. In the 1700s, successful doctoring was often due more to luck than to skill. Although almost every militia regiment had its own doctor, called the regimental surgeon,

*A satirical view of conditions in a
hospital of the colonial era*

he was more often than not poorly trained and rarely prepared to treat battle wounds. These doctors, as well as the civilian physicians of the day, knew very little about the causes of illness and the successful treatment of infections. Bloodletting, blistering, and purging were the usual treatments for every ailment from simple headaches to smallpox and gunshot wounds. For pain relief medical satchels contained mainly laudanum (a specific remedy made of opium and alcohol), wine, herbs, and root extracts.

Women in colonial homes were responsible for tending the sick and the injured and most ill people preferred the herbal medicines and "old wives" remedies to the often painful and generally unsuccessful practices of physicians. Women learned about healing from their mothers and by reading recipe books. When colonial women spoke of "recipes" they usually meant the directions for making medicines, not for preparing food.

Mary, like many colonial women, could read and write, although more could read than write. Next to the Bible, medical texts were the most popular reading for women. Family survival depended on their ability to deliver babies and care for the ill and wounded.

Both doctors and colonial women faced the nearly constant life-threatening epidemics that often spread through a city or town with amazing speed. Smallpox was the principal disease at the time of the Revolutionary War. George Washington had his wife and his troops pox-proofed against this dread disease, and in 1777, he required the civilian population of Morristown, New Jersey, to be treated to help prevent the spread of the disease to his wintering troops. Another serious disease was typhus, then called hospital or jail fever. Dysentery also plagued the soldiers, as did yellow fever and scarlet fever.

If a soldier happened to survive these and other diseases, he faced the hazards of war and gunshot or cannonball wounds. Even a superficial wound was taken seriously by army surgeons. Removing a ball from a wound was usually done with a probe such as forceps, or if necessary, the surgeon stuck his finger into the wound to find and remove the ball. Scraps of uniform cloth and splinters carried into the wound with the ball caused infection and the resulting gangrene meant amputation. If wounded in a body part that couldn't be amputated, the soldier faced a prolonged period of illness which ended either in death or recovery.

The wounded British officer arrived at the parsonage in very poor condition due to a gunshot. Although constantly aware that he is the enemy, Mary is genuinely concerned for him and relieves his suffering as well as she can. Her generous spirit and her medical skills were not that unusual, however. Colonial women generally took good care of

An eighteenth-century medicine chest,
with instruments, drug packets, and bottles

enemy soldiers because they hoped that the same would be done for their husbands if they were wounded.

Mary writes of her feelings and those of her family, neighbors, and friends during the long period of the British soldier's illness. She spent much time trying to take his mind off his pain, talking with him and reading to him by the hour. With time, a deep friendship evolved between Mary and the major, who stayed at the parsonage from December 1776 to June 1778. It is their unusual friendship that helps Mary come through the ordeal of the occupation and her husband's long absence.

December, 1776

An officer of high rank is in winter quarters with us; resistance is out of the question; wounded and ill, we deeply sympathize with him. Foe or friend, he must be cared for compassionately.

Tuesday, December, 1776

Major Musgrave has two servants. They attend upon him assiduously, but we can minister to the mind of the gentleman, and by reading and conversing, can beguile him sometimes of the thought of his situation.

Oh, dear husband, war is a weariness! Its effects sicken the soul. Every hour some fresh account of murder, robbery, wounding, destroying, depredating! When will this unnatural warfare be at an end?

Wednesday, 1776

Major Musgrave is very ill to-day, but yet considerate, and full of the thoughtful courtesy of the gentleman. What a blessed thing it is, that national animosity can be lost sight of, forgotten, in sorrow and compassion for a fellow creature's distress! It leads me constantly to bring home to my own thoughts and feelings the idea of a beloved husband, child, or brother, in such a situation, away from me and all that he loved; amid those against whom his hand had been raised in warfare; wounded, ill, in pain, and anguish of spirit. Should I not cherish, in the deep places of my heart, an everlasting gratitude? And should I not teach it religiously to my children, to those who had *thus* ministered to mine own?

Monday, December, 1776

The neighbors feel in Major Musgrave an involuntary interest. Sympathy forms this bond. They call often to see him, and inquire about him, and bring nice things to tempt the sick man's appetite. Such attentions touch him sensibly. The wound is very bad; it has induced a high fever. He is patient and uncomplaining, which is ten times more touching than if he were cross and irritable.

The next entry in the journal refers to the mental suffering of the major. Mary notes that the major seems to be able to bear the physical pain better than the mental anguish he suffers. As you will read later in this chapter, the mental pain is caused by a lost love, one that permanently affected his life. Mary's romantic heart is touched by the officer's courage.

Tuesday, December, 1776

I cannot but be powerfully moved by the wounded man who lies below. His heroic patience in such deep suffering is to be greatly admired; also his consideration of others in the midst of it. He seems to forget himself, in the fear of giving trouble and inconvenience. My father says it is the gift of God—Grace, which enables him to triumph over the pains of the body. I asked Major Musgrave if he had always endured suffering so patiently? He replied, "I have not borne mental trials with patience or meekness; they are more difficult to endure than bodily pain." He has before made allusion to some great sorrow which he has experienced.

Thursday, January, 1777

The Major is rather better, the wound appears to be healing, but he is miserably weak and ill. I went into his room to-day rather unexpectedly; he appeared to have a miniature [a small portrait] in his hand and put it hastily aside. I asked no questions, of course.

Winter, Thursday, 1777

The army in winter quarters at Morristown. Depredation and destruction going on here.

Major Musgrave sits up an hour or two every day;

A miniature from the Revolutionary era

he powerfully awakens my sympathy. Do not be frightened, my husband. Pity, admiration of his patient endurance, no other sentiment can animate my breast. He is our country's foe, but circumstances have made him so; and he said to me this day, "It is a wicked war, and if it please God to raise me up, I shall never again engage in it."

Wednesday, August, 1777

Major Musgrave seems very feeble; it is doubtful whether he survives the winter. It is affecting to see him, he is so weak and helpless, yet patient and uncomplaining. On going to his room to-day, he appeared to be reading old letters, and was evidently much moved. I took up Bishop Jeremy Taylor's "Holy Living and Dying," which my father so delighteth in, and asked whether I should read to him. He assented gratefully, and I read an appropriate comforting passage.

January, 1778

Major Musgrave still lingers. I found him very weak to-day, but in no pain, for which I desire to be thankful. He appeareth very sad at times; was so to-day. I tried to soothe and comfort him again that I would attend to all of his wishes; write a particular account to his mother, whom he fondly loves, of his last words, of his constant consideration and thoughtfulness of others, his patience, and of his hope of pardon and peace, vouchsafed to him in the holy calm and perfect reliance which he is often favored to experience.

Mary's journal illustrates that life and loving do go on, even in wartime and in the face of death. An entry tells of both the joy of joining two young people who are filled with love in marriage, and the fears for what the future will hold for this young couple. Mary contrasts the happy young couple with the deep sadness she sees in the face of the young British officer.

Jan. 10th, 1778

What extremes there are in life!

Robert Adams came last night to ask father to unite him to Rose Wilson. It is strange to see two happy faces amid violence, gloom, and destruction. I was saddened when I thought how soon the joy beaming there would be clouded over in these stormy times. But when my father, whose heart is full of heavenly grace, pronounced his benediction upon the young, hopeful couple, mine responded a deep "Amen."

Marcia went into the other room, and picked two white rosebuds off her bush, and some geranium leaves, which she tied up and gave to the sweet bride, who in purity and grace could almost vie with the flowers.

The ceremony was performed in Major Musgrave's room, at his request. He was much affected, and gave them at parting a gold piece, and the blessing, he said, of a dying man.

After they departed, Major Musgrave said to me, "Madam, will you do me the favor to sit with me a while? I would unburden my mind while I have the strength, and make a few requests of you."

"As regards the war," said Major Musgrave, after some conversations on other topics, "I will say to you, I regret having ever engaged in it; and had it pleased God to have spared my life, it was my determination to have retired from the service."

I was surprised to hear this avowal, for a more loyal subject of King George, and dearer lover of England, cannot be found. Major Musgrave proceeded to say that it was a most wicked and unnatural war. "The very idea," said he, "of shooting down men who speak the same language and own a common origin, is monstrous. My share in it hath pierced me with sorrow.

"I shall never be able," he continued, "to show the sincerity of my repentance; but, my dear madam, I speak the truth before the Searcher of hearts. You will believe this, my solemn assertion. Time is drawing to a close. It hath pleased God to try me and gift me sorely in this life. I have grievously rebelled against his will; have murmured, have mourned, have wept, have agonized. My spirit hath beat so long and unremittingly against the bars of the prisonhouse, that at last it sinks weak and powerless. And it is in this passive, childlike state, that the first germs of daybreak, the first faint whispers of hope and peace, have visited me. And yet the strength is wanting now, to sing the praise and thanksgiving."

I was awed to witness the devotional state of mind to which divine grace had brought Major Musgrave.

He continued.

"And now, my dearest lady, how can I express my overflowing gratitude to you?"

My heart leaped at this noble acknowledgement of the little we had done. I assured him that we should be rejoiced, and amply repaid, to feel assured that we had alleviated one pang, or beguiled one hour of his suffering mind and body. And when I remember, dear Edward, the day the poor wounded man was brought here, how troubled and willing to be rid of the charge I was, conscience smote me, and I felt that I deserved no thanks. The edifying contemplation of such patient sorrow and unselfishness is worth purchasing at ten times the inconvenience.

Major Musgrave continued.

"I have one request to make, which I trust your honored father will not be displeased with. It is that my body may be laid in the Friends' burial-place. The desire I have expressed will prove the influence which their principles have obtained upon my mind; my admiration of opinions so new to me is great. The neighboring family, the Pattison family, do so beautifully enforce and exemplify them, the head of it especially. I have, and shall ever venerate the Church of England, the church of my forefathers, of my mother. But the peaceful tenets of this simple people come home so to my state, shedding such balm and repose over a wounded spirit, that I trust the desire to find a last resting-place with them will be regarded."

He requested that the service for the burial of the dead should be read at his grave.

I assured Major Musgrave of my sympathy and appreciation of his feelings. Nor do I think this change to be wondered at in one fresh from witnessing and experiencing, in his own person, the sickening horrors and dreadful evils of War. My own wretched suspense and anxiety doubtless has its influence. I am trying to *write down thought*, to beguile myself a little while of miserable fears.

The Major placed in my hands a manuscript. He said he had written it for my perusal, wishing to acquaint me with his past experience; but feeling too acutely still to do so verbally. He requested me to present his watch to my father, gave a valuable ring containing a brilliant to me, and a memento to each of the children. His consideration and composure were so sweet and touching, that they affected me, and I could not refrain from tears.

I hastily quitted the room, fearing to excite my dear friend, and knowing that he required rest.

Monday Morning

Oh, my dear husband, it is a mournful thing to contemplate! A man full of gently courtesy, of sensitive and shrinking delicacy, receiving at the hands of strangers, in the attitude of their enemy, all of the sympathy or earthly support that he can receive in his dying moments! It grieves me inexpressibly. In such circumstances all animosity of a public nature is completely swallowed up. It must be heart of stone that is not moved, melted to pity!

The day that Mary has known for some time would come now arrived. Major Musgrave finally died of complications from his battle wounds. In a letter to her husband she expresses great regret for the officer's death. She reminds her husband that Major Musgrave had requested burial in the Friends' graveyard and that he will most likely be the only soldier ever to be buried there. Since the members of the Society of Friends do not believe in making war or participating in combat, she is undoubtedly correct. The man named Shultz who is mentioned in this letter is the Major's aide who was also quartered at the parsonage.

Monday, June 16th, 1778

Major Musgrave is no more.

His conflict is over, and he sleepeth in peace.

My father had been much with him during the day. He was distressed at times with the difficulty of breathing. In an interval of quiet he [my father] read to him the beautiful Visitation of the Sick. Those comfortable words seemed like the dew to the parched herbage; his soul drank them in and was refreshed. In an hour after he fell asleep, and we thought the summons might be delayed some time longer; but at midnight I was called by Shultz. I went quickly; but when I leaned over the bedside to catch the faintest whisper, the dying man tried to speak but could not. He pressed my hand, and raised his eyes to heaven; this action, and the ineffably grateful expression of his countenance said, as plainly as words could, "God bless you!"

Major Musgrave had become so near in sympathy and interest to us all, that it seemed like the loss of a dear friend.

It costs us some effort to obey his injunction as

regardeth his last resting place. It seems to my father a strange request; but it shall be sacred.

Thursday Evening

The body was to-day laid in the green burial ground, near the meeting house of the Friends. It was followed to the place by three companies of soldiers, marching to the solemn music and the muffled drum.

The sublime and impressive words of the Burial Service were read by my dear father. How they appeared to awe every one!

"Man that is born of a woman hath but a short time to live, and is full of misery. He cometh up and is cut down like a flower; he fleeth as it were a shadow; and never continueth in one stay."

These words convey a mournful lesson, but those which follow are full of hope.

"I heard a voice from heaven saying unto me, Write from henceforth, Blessed are the dead who die in the Lord (in faith and love to Him); Even so, saith the Spirit; for they rest from their labors."

The firing over the dead, awakening thoughts of strife and battle, was in painful contrast to these life-giving words. The echoes of that peaceful spot had never before been thus awakened. Though many soldiers of the cross lie there, this is the first, and likely to be the only, instance on record, of a soldier of earthly combat and carnal weapons taking there his last rest.

There is no stone to mark the spot; but a young tree growing near. I know it, and my thoughts will often visit it.

Summer, Saturday, 1778

I have been employed to-day in putting up with great care everything belonging to Major Musgrave, that they may be sent, when occasion offers, to his friends in England. In a little box of spice wood (of which he gave me the key) I found a packet of letters and papers left for the perusal, and put them away for some future time. Recollection is too fresh now.

The consciousness that my feeble efforts were made to assuage his grief (and it is my conviction that Major Musgrave's sorrows were deeper than met the eye), to smooth his passage to the tomb, and to comfort his last hours with sympathy and care, is full of inward peace and satisfaction.

Fall, 1780

I regret, dear Edward, that you never knew Major Musgrave; I am sure that your discriminating judgment would have led you to appreciate him.

We still feel his loss deeply. Even Charles, though young and volatile, was saddened many days after his departure, as were the servants, and every one about the house.

The following entry appears in the journal, although the author was Major Musgrave, who kept his own journal while he was at the parsonage. He specified that Mary was to have the journal and his other private papers after he died; that they were not to be sent to England.

Mary puts off reading the Major's papers until the time when she feels his words will make his death less painful for her. Then she suggests that her husband, Edward, also read some of the major's words so that he, too, would eventually come to admire the man who became her friend.

Because his suffering is so intense, Major Musgrave's mind wanders in and out of reality from time to time, with the result that his journal rambles and is confusing. For clarity's sake, we have summarized the story of his life and why he came to be in America at the time of the Revolution. It is a tale of love and betrayal.

Besides his widowed mother, the Major had a brother and an orphaned cousin living in his home in England.

He compares himself to his cousin Howard, describing the cousin as a running, leaping impulsive young man, while he himself was studious and quiet—a romantic who loved stories of enchantment and the lore of chivalry and knighthood.

Howard, two years older, entered the Royal Navy in hope of seeing the world. While he was off on His Majesty's ships, Musgrave fell in love with young, beautiful Grace Arden. Although they had known each other for many years, he only realized he was in love with Grace when she went away to school. Grace decided that she was in love with him, too, after he declared himself, and they were supremely happy. Then Howard came home from his ship in the Mediterranean.

Howard arrived in his dashing uniform and swept Grace off her feet. But she couldn't find a way to tell Musgrave that she loved his cousin Howard and not him, so she said nothing. Musgrave learned the truth only when two letters arrived at the same time at his apartment in London. One letter was addressed to Howard and the other to him. Unfortunately, Grace accidentally (or perhaps on purpose) switched the envelopes and Musgrave got the letter meant for Howard. In this letter, Grace dwelt on her love for Howard and wrote of not wanting to hurt Musgrave's feelings. Musgrave, shocked and distraught, became physically ill. He asked his mother to come to London so he would not be alone. He then decided to join the army and leave Grace and England forever.

From the manuscript of Major Musgrave:

"London would not hold me now, nor England. I must go somewhere. My mother suggested the Continent. New scenes and travel, she felt sure, would in time restore me to my wanted cheerfulness. Oh, little my mother knew of the spirit wound I had received!

"The revolt of the American Colonies had broken out. It was the field for me. I knew I must have action;

it was the only escape from the thoughts which assailed me, the phantom of the past which pursued and tormented without ceasing.

"It was a dreadful separation to my mother. If a mother ever feels an intenser love for one child than for another, mine did for me; a son after her own heart, dependent on her for sympathy, even when a child, and as a man, trustful, confiding, and affectionate. Besides, was I not now the object of her deep commiseration? The tenderest emotions of the heart flowed out to me in near and embracing sympathy.

"I cannot recur the parting scene. Having obtained a commission of rank in the army, I embarked for the Colonies. Here I have been struggling with fate three long years. You, my dear [Mary], have seen the end. Your tears fall. You weep that one so young should be the victim of unrestrained passion. It *is* sorrowful *thus* to die. But Death, I hail thee as a merciful messenger! I know that I am in the hands of One who knoweth and pitieth my infirmities. He will have mercy on me. All my pangs, my struggles, are not hid from him. He heareth the voice of my prayer. Blessed be his holy name!

"Send the other keepsakes to my precious mother. My heart aches for her in anticipation of the anguish she will have on my account! God bless her! And you, my dear lady, your honored father, and the little ones. You have all solaced and comforted me."

7

THEY ALSO SERVE WHO ONLY STAND AND WAIT

THE SECOND AND THIRD AMENDMENTS to the Constitution concerned ideas that were extremely important to the Americans of the Revolutionary War period, but seem less important to Americans today. Nowadays in the United States, for example, soldiers are not likely to be assigned to live in people's houses. The Third Amendment states: No soldier shall, in time of peace, be quartered in any house without the consent of the owner; nor in time of war but in a manner to be prescribed by law.

Historians differ as to the meaning of the Second Amendment. In the late 1700s the militia was the country's chief defense. A militia is an army made up of citizens trained for war or any other emergency. During the colonial period, every colony had its own militia. Today every state maintains a militia but in each it is called the National Guard. If the actual wording of this amendment reflected the concern of colonial Americans about the militia, today's citizens have taken a broader interpretation of the Second Amendment. Does the amendment protect an individual's right to own a firearm to protect life and personal property, or is it still meant primarily to protect only the collective right of the people to defend their state?

A well-regulated militia, being necessary to the security of a free state, the right of the people to keep and bear arms may not be infringed.

As you read Mary's words about her experiences and those of the other Long Islanders who were pushed into war whether they chose to take an active part or not, try to envision the dangers they encountered, the hardships they endured, and the rejoicing they made whenever the Patriots avoided serious defeats during the long years of war. Although she clearly chose the Patriot side and helped to run the farm while her husband was away, Mary did not take an active part in the Revolution as did, say, Deborah Sampson, who, disguised as a man, fought in several battles before being wounded. Nor did she take her husband's place in battle, as did Margaret Corbin of Pennsylvania when her husband was killed.

Like many other American Patriot women, Mary worked at keeping her family safe while her husband was at war, nursing the wounded and sick (even enemy soldiers), occasionally hiding fugitive Patriots, and rejuvenating the spirits of her husband through her comforting letters to him.

Saturday, Nov. 27, 1776

Received a few hasty lines from White Plains. They mention an engagement on the 28th October; "retreated with loss." I cannot but feel despondent. *Where is it to end, and how?* The army is greatly reduced by killed, wounded, and taken, and those whose enlistments have expired daily leaving; the poor creatures remaining, many without shoes or comfortable clothing, are sadly disheartened. The enemy have possession of the city of New York, of Staten Island, and of Long Island. Who can look without trembling at the failure of this struggle to throw off our yoke? The reins drawn tighter, more oppressed and circumscribed, and the examples made of rebels—it is fearful to think of.

It must have been an affecting sight to witness the enthusiasm of the poor, barefooted, ragged, hungry troops, tossing up their crownless hats in the air, when on his white charger, the general rode into camp!

I will confess a womanly admiration of a noble exterior. Washington's influence and authority must be enhanced by his gallant bearing and commanding figure, as he sits his proud steed.

You never look at the possibility of failure. It is the cause of liberty, the cause of humanity; yet your letter breathes discouragement. We are so far separated, there is so much uncertainty; and war is so sorrowful, that I sometimes feel a longing to fly with you to a place of peace and safety.

Adieu! The little ones are well.

Your fond and foreboding wife.

December, 1776

General Howe has issued a proclamation offering pardon to all who will submit to royal authority. Pardon! For what? A just indignation against rights trampled upon!

It is said that many wealthy and influential persons have deserted the American cause. It is indeed a gloomy hour! But we *must* triumph. The descendants of those who sought here a peaceful asylum from oppression—Huguenots, Puritans, Covenanters [Scottish Presbyterians]—will not submit to oppression here. They will defend it with their lives. The ocean rolled between them and their tyrants, *then*, as it will *again.* It is God's decree that this people shall be free. The broad lands of the new continent are destined for all time to be the asylum of the Persecuted, the Poor, the Suffering! Tyranny here shall never hold his baleful sway!

Thursday, December, 1776

To-day little Marcia found me weeping over your miniature. She took it out of my hand, and covering it with kisses, said, "Oh, that is my dear papa. He is a brave man, is he not, mamma? And the best man too that ever lived. When will he come back?"

This prattle will be sweet to your ears, for it comes from the heart.

March 6th, 1777

Spring is again opening, and the war seems just begun!

A young French nobleman has arrived, having embraced voluntarily the American cause; the love of freedom, and a desire to succor the oppressed, were his only incentives. The Marquis de la Fayette has been appointed a Major-General. He is not twenty years of age. A man of wealth, and used to the luxury of a court.

Our cause assumes consequence in the eyes of foreign powers. Even poor Major Musgrave speaks with greater moderation of probable success in quelling "the revolt."

March, 1777

I long for the hastening of the day when "the nations shall not learn war any more, nor lift up sword against nation; but the sword shall be turned into the ploughshare, and the spear into the pruning hook."

I suppose you will say, "So be it"—after our independence is secured!

Tuesday, May 1st, 1777

Our vines are putting forth; the grass is springing; all nature has put on her lovely garb of green. The children are full of joy; it is difficult to keep them to their tasks; but through the long winter they have been more industrious. Charles is quite proficient in study, his grandpa thinks. I hope you may not have reason to be ashamed of him. This weary absence maketh sick the heart; but I will not dwell upon the sad subject; it pains you to hear me repine. I trust God in his providence will so order the course of events, that all will work together for good. I will try to bear without murmuring whatever He in his wisdom may send.

"They also serve who only stand and wait."

In her next entry Mary writes of the colonial alliance with France and how happy she is to learn of it. Of all possible foreign friendships for her new country, France was both the most promising and the most powerful.

After the American victory at Saratoga, Burgoyne surrendered his entire army, still nearly 5,500 strong, to the Patriots. France, which had secretly been helping the colonial forces with money and supplies, decided to come out openly on the side of the colonies.

As a result, the United States and France entered into a treaty of alliance in 1778. This treaty was largely the work of Benjamin Franklin. Under the terms of the treaty of alliance, France agreed to fight on the side of the Americans until full independence was achieved. Through the alliance the beleaguered rebels received subsidies which amounted to nearly $62 million dollars, and a series of loans which totaled over $6 million.

The French were, of course, interested in getting something in return for their assistance. As the French Foreign

Benjamin Franklin, sent by Congress to the French court, won money, supplies, and the support of the French navy for the American cause.

Benjamin Franklin L.L.D.
Envoy from the American Congress to the French Court.

Minister, Count de Vergennes commented, "The power that first recognizes the independence of the Americans will be the one that will reap the fruits of war." Regardless of the strings attached to the French assistance, the alliance gave Mary and her fellow Patriots cause for great rejoicing, although, in Mary's case, she also feels her father's distress at the news. By this time, many Americans were growing restless under the restrictions and privations of wartime. They yearned for an end to war and suffering.

Tuesday, January, 1778

Just received the joyful news of the Treaty of Alliance with France. My heart beats tremulously with hope and expectation, and yet I scarcely know what to hope for. Can I, a woman, wife, and mother, delight in warfare, or desire the destruction of the children of common origin? No! May God of his merciful goodness grant a speedy termination of the war! This be my prevailing, my fervent prayer.

It is thought the news of General Burgoyne's surrender decided the negotiations, by giving strong encouragement.

My father is very quiet about the news; he longs for peace, but cannot turn against his native England. He loves her with all her provocation, or in spite of it.

Tuesday, Late Summer, 1778

I received, dearest Edward, to-day, your charming letter of the 15th of August.

The arrival of the French fleet, twelve ships of the line and four frigates, under command of Count d'Estaigne, is joyful news.

The British troops remain inactive in New York since the battle of Monmouth. The American loss that day was small; but the great heat occasioned many deaths, and much grievous suffering in both armies.

I look forward to the day with trembling eagerness when all shall be over, and we shall rest in enjoyment of the peace so dearly bought; for though *you*, my dear Edward, never stopped to count the cost, when you enlisted life, limb, and fortune in the cause. *I* cannot help thinking sometimes, in my desponding moments, that the risk of life and limb, neglect of affairs, loss of property, of health, of ease, of comfort, is the tremendous price of liberty. You say, "she is worth ten times as many sacrifices, if could be, than these even." She may be to those surviving to enjoy and reap her laurels, but patriotism in *my* breast, just now, is too faint a spark of glory in perspective, in a hero's memory, though embalmed in tears!

It seemeth too dear at such a price. Bear with me, my husband; you know I am sorely tried. I will strive for more patience and submission, and commit thy precious life to the care of Him, without whom not a sparrow falleth to the ground.

Sunday, 1781

An unusual press for men and horses to-day. The Sabbath is no more regarded than any other day, especially as it affords a favorable time for stealing hay, cattle, etc., when most of the men are attending divine worship.

Being at private devotions I was interrupted by the entrance of Charles, shouting vociferously, "The Britisher is after Nero!"

It seems that a light-horseman rode up to Henry Pattison's inquiring for men; all were gone to meeting. He looked about and in the house, and satisfied himself, but unfortunately espied Nero [a black servant who worked for Mary's father] standing in the stable doorway.

"By Jove," said he, "I'll have that Negro."

Seeing the soldier running toward him, poor Nero

expected to be taken, and was already trying to reconcile himself to his fate, but he suddenly thought, "It's not worthwhile to give in without an effort." So keeping the barn between himself and his pursuer, he made for a large haystack enclosed in the middle of the field.

The redcoat ran his horse violently, with the intention, doubtless, of overtaking him before he reached the stack; but Nero, though rather old and stiff, reached it, and jumped over the fence of enclosure.

Almost instantly the Britisher rode up with his drawn sword, and swore if he did not yield himself up, he would run him through.

We now saw the soldier ride furiously round the haystack, and old Nero get on it, although with some difficulty, for it was ten or fifteen feet high. Then the enemy dismounted and leaped over the fence. Nero running backwards and forwards on the haystack (the top of it was flat and about thirty feet long) the soldier striking at him unsuccessfully with his sword all the time. At length we saw that he too got upon the haystack, and we gave up poor Nero; his fate seemed inevitable. Not so, he most adroitly eluded the lighthorseman; jumped off, crossed the fence, and made for the woods.

His pursuer meanwhile mounted his horse and was in hot pursuit; indeed, close at his heels. Luckily there was a thick hedge to cross, where our old Nero had the advantage, for the horse would not leap it, and the rider, fuming and cursing dreadfully, was obliged to dismount again; but the fugitive was now far on his way to the woods, where it was fruitless to follow. He was in such a rage at being thus baffled, that Nero would have fared badly had he ever fallen into his hands. He remained in the woods until dark, when he crept home, and received a warm welcome, especially from the children.

8
THE WAR COMES TO AN END

AS MARY NOTES IN HER JOURNAL, each side in the American Revolution had a strategy for winning the war. The British strategy had three parts: to drive a wedge between the northern and southern colonies and keep them separated, to defeat the Americans in battle after battle and wear them down, and to control the important colonial cities. On the other hand, the Patriot strategy was simply to avoid serious defeats and to prolong the war long enough for the French to come in and help them, and for the British people to get tired of the war. In the end, the American strategy proved successful. The British defeat at Saratoga, New York, meant that the British would not be able to separate New England from the rest of the colonies. France actively joined the American side. So did Spain, and then England and the Netherlands went to war against each other. With so much trouble facing them in Europe, the English people began to lose interest in the war in America, and started talking about peace.

While peace talks were beginning, the fighting continued in America. When the British failed to cut off New England, they turned their attention to the South. Lord Cornwallis, hoping to lead his troops through Virginia and cut the colonies in two, landed a large force at Yorktown, Virginia, and waited for help from the British forces in New York City. Before that help arrived, however, French naval forces blocked the harbor. Cornwallis was not able to retreat by sea and he could not move on land either, because American and French armies commanded by George Washington surrounded him and had him trapped. On October 19, 1781, Lord Cornwallis surrendered. The British government, thoroughly discouraged by the surrender and realizing it was hopeless to try any longer to control the colonies, decided to accept the independence of the American colonies. At a peace conference in Paris in 1783, the British government recognized the United States as an independent nation. Mary wrote of many of these momentous events in her journal. And when we read about these events in her own words, she helps us to see what the struggle meant for the people who lived during those times. The hardships they had to bear made the American victory over the British army all the more impressive.

Winter, 1778
Monday

A scene took place at neighbor Pattison's the day before the redcoats left, which I will note down for your amusement; for when the battles are fought, the victory won, and we sit down beneath our own vine and fig tree, to join together these pages, we will weep and smile over them, and bless Heaven that the trials and dangers are past.

Well, Edith hath been sadly persecuted of late by one of the officers, Captain Morton. And I am of the opinion that she would rather favor his suit, if he were anything but a soldier; but love will not run away with her judgment. He is a high-spirited, noble-looking young man, and desperately in love with Edith, which surely is not to be wondered at. Being constantly in her train in their time of leisure, several gentlemen have become enamored of her.

On this occasion she was in the sitting room, spinning. I heard that Captain Morton had said that he would waste all day to see Edith spin. Indeed she does look serenely beautiful, and stately, as with measured though light step, she throws the great wheel, while her delicate fingers hold the slender thread.

The wheel as it goes round makes a monotonous, sad sound which I love to hear. So often when Bridget [a servant in the parsonage] spins, I open the door of the upper room, that the sound thereof may reach me below, where I sit sewing, or teaching the children. It reminds me of the fall winds among the withered leaves, or the distant sound of rushing waters.

Well, I doubt not Edith was enjoying her own pure and peaceful thoughts, when Captain Morton entered the room. She was grieved to see him, thinking and consoling herself that he had wholly left these parts, in that she heard no tidings of him for many days.

He began abruptly to speak, saying,

"Edith, you have not seen me for some time, in accordance with your wish; I have been making trial of my power of self-control. Look at me; behold my success!"

She directed her attention to the young man, and was struck with the change which was manifest in his appearance. From the handsome, fine-looking Britisher that he was, he had become pale, stooping, and hollow-eyed.

"Give me hope, or I die; some word of comfort; a look or tone of love; some promise for my thoughts to feed on, to sustain me in absence. Tomorrow with this precious boon I go; without it, this is my resource."

Thus saying, the desperate young man took his

pistol from his side, and pointed it at his breast. Edith was terrified, but preserving that quietness of manner which belongs to the people of their sect, she left her wheel, and gently, but firmly, took the pistol out of his hand, and laid it aside.

The officer made no resistance; but seemed as though beneath a spell. The spell was the serene sweetness and composure of her demeanor.

"The intemperance thou showest," said Edith, "would intimidate me from forming any closer intimacy with thee. Besides, how dost thou think it would seem to my parents and to Friends, that I should contract an engagement with one who holds it no wrong to lift up sword against his fellow man?"

"Edith, do not set down against me that in which I had no control. Am I to be blamed for being bred to the profession of arms, that I am become the instrument of power to suppress the rebel colonies? The members of your Society are generally supposed to be in the side of the Mother Country."

"It is true," said Edith, "they *are* called *Tories*, but unjustly, as they espouse neither cause. From their great principle, 'Resist not evil,' and submission to the powers that be, they are opposed to the rising of the people against the Mother Country."

(Her father, I have a strong suspicion, wishes, though very cautious, success to the cause of freedom.)

Captain Morton said, "You surely, Edith, wish to see the rebellion quelled, and order and quiet restored?"

"I desire peace most fervently, but you, our brethren, have oppressed us wrongfully, trodden upon our rights, and domineered over us until patience hath had her perfect work, and seemeth to be no longer a virtue. And I will venture to predict that the side which so wise, so temperate, so just a man as George

Washington leads, will be the successful one. Heaven will smile upon it."

The captain was certainly surprised at this earnest ebullition [outburst] of feeling, and disappointed too. But his love overbears all, and makes him take rebuke, from Edith most patiently.

He said he would reflect upon her remarks; his hopes seemed to have risen; why, she knew not. He took her hand in his, and pressed it to his lips. She promised to remember him with kindness, and they parted.

She will doubtless hear from him again, which I think she will not regret.

This young officer's love for Edith led him to remain in America after independence was achieved, and, in the course of time, and through her influence, he became a constant member of the Society of Friends, and her beloved, and loving husband.

May 5th, 1778

The British Ministry begins to speak of American affairs with more moderation. It is probably the effect of the fate of their Northern Army and the Alliance with France. Lord North laid before Parliament bills for conciliation, and commissioners are appointed to bring terms of accommodation. The day is past for that. Two years ago perhaps reconciliation might have been effected; but we are too sanguine of success, to admit now of listening to any terms but acknowledgment of our independence.

October, 1780
Tuesday

In reading my Bible today I came to that beautiful passage: "And nation shall not lift up sword against nation, nor learn war anymore. The sword shall be turned into the ploughshare, and the spear into the pruning hook." It appears to indicate that the peaceful pursuits of agriculture will prevail over the earth, and war and devastation cease. May God hasten the day!

Thursday

No news of importance. A deputation of Friends was sent last month to a place called Nine Partners, about twenty miles east of the Hudson River. Henry Pattison was one of the number; he gives a very interesting account of their progress. They crossed the water to Mamaroneck, and proceeded to White Plains. They had some questioning to undergo from the enemy, as they were obliged to pass the Continental lines; and coming from Long Island, where the British power is supreme, they had fears of being stopped; still, believing themselves to be within their religious duty, they persevered. They passed near General Washington's headquarters. On approaching, they were stopped, examined severely, and handed over to the Committee of Safety, which declared they could not allow them to proceed consistently with the orders they had received.

They then desired that General Washington might be informed of their detention, and requested that he would give them an interview. It was granted. They were received with marked deference and respect. It is the custom of this peculiar sect to speak with moderation, never in strong terms, complimentary language being specially disapproved of. But I can gather from their quaint though guarded phrase, that they were much struck with the elegance and dignity of General Washington's person and address.

Friend Pattison admitted that he was a likely man, and conducted himself with great propriety. As much praise as they could be expected to bestow upon "a fighting character."

106

After politely requesting them to be seated, the General made close inquiry relating to the British force on the island.

His manner being calculated to inspire confidence, they very candidly told all they knew, and acquainted him with some facts before unknown to him.

General Washington inquired where they passed the night, and said he was entirely convinced, from his knowledge of their Society, and of the person with whom they tarried, that their object was, as they represented, entirely religious. He apologized for their detention, saying it seemed unavoidable, and if they returned the same way, he should be happy to hear of their success in seeing their friends.

When the humble company entered the General's presence, an aide stepped up, and hinted to them the propriety of removing their hats.

Henry Pattison said, "In presence of God in prayer alone, do we bow the uncovered head. Before kings, or the mightiest of earth's potentates, this respect is not shown. In *His* sight there is no respect of persons; in ours, all men are brethren."

General Washington said he was well acquainted with their customs, and some of his best friends were of their body. He advised them to go forward, and always plainly tell the truth.

On their return, passing again near the camp, they availed themselves of General Washington's invitation. He appeared deeply interested in their relation of what they had seen and heard, and dismissed them with kind assurances of regard, requesting them to represent to the enemy whatever they chose, as he knew they would tell only the truth, in which he was willing to trust.

Mary's next entry tells of a rumor of an important Colonial victory in the southern states. At this time she is not able to find out if the story is true or not. We know now that after 1778 most of the fighting took place in the South. The British sent Lord Cornwallis to conquer the South. He captured Savannah and took all of Georgia. He also captured Charlestown, South Carolina, and a colonial army of 5,618 soldiers. But she has learned that General Washington's armies have left the North and are reportedly heading south. The patriots in the South fought for the most part in small bands of militiamen. They played "hide and seek" with the British. In this way they kept the British following them away from the seacoast. They stopped Cornwallis at King's Mountain, North Carolina, forcing him back to Wilmington. Then, when he moved up to Yorktown, Washington had his chance to trap Cornwallis. The French fleet sailed into Chesapeake Bay, beat the British fleet, and cut off Cornwallis's escape by sea.

But all this is still in the future. As far as Mary is concerned, she and her fellow Islanders have enough trouble with the criminals roaming the region. With all the armies gone from the area, she and her neighbors are once again vulnerable to attack by robbers and looters.

August, 1780
Thursday

There is a rumor of a great battle fought at the South, and the Continentals [American Continental army] victorious. I cannot vouch for the truth of it. My first thought and prayer is my husband's safety; the next for our country.

By skillful military maneuvers, General Washington has kept Sir Henry Clinton in a state of continual alarm and uncertainty for some time. It was generally understood that New York was the point of attack. But the General suddenly broke up the camp at White Plains, and crossed the Hudson river.

The house of Fry Willis, of Jericho, was entered by way of the kitchen, where a young man and woman were sitting over the fire. The robbers fired off a gun to obtain a light. They then set a guard over each bed, and searched for money and valuables. The man servant, "a warrior," attempted to run for his sword, but was held back. They ransacked cabinets, desks, etc., and took money to a considerable amount, the serving man's excepted, which was concealed under a drawer.

The robbers, on entering the house of John Willis, were so exasperated at the finding of no booty, that they tied the hands of all the family behind them, as well as those of the eminent preacher, Joseph Delapaine, who was their guest at the time.

They dragged the wife of Mr. Willis by the hair about the house, and then left them, telling them that they had set fire to the house, which was true, as they saw the flames kindling and curling up the wooden jamb beside the fireplace. Their hands were tied!

A young woman named Phebe Powell, by dint of the most powerful efforts, at length loosened one of her hands and ran to extinguish the flames, which she succeeded in doing before releasing the rest from their thongs.

January 1st

It is the first day of the year. The little ones are very merry, and are wishing all they meet "a happy coming year." It is for them a pleasant day, but we are saddened by its recurrence. The sunshine of their hearts is not clouded; blessed season of hope and joy! In my own, too, it dawns more brightly than the last. My loved partner is not here, but I have cause to sing the song of deliverance, in that his precious life hath been preserved amid so many and great dangers, which he has never shunned but rather courted. Is not the prospect brightened for my country since this time last year? And for him whom the voice of men placed at the helm—the great Washington—is there no joy, no gratitude, in the deep places of my heart, that God hath raised him up, hath preserved, hath prospered him?

Officers from several foreign countries helped the colonies during the American Revolution. In fact, the Continental army eagerly enlisted the support of Europeans in the war against England. From Prussia came Baron Friedrich von Steuben, a captain in the Prussian army. Von Steuben was a fine drillmaster who Benjamin Franklin felt would be able to turn the untrained Continental soldiers into a fighting army. Von Steuben was a cheerful man with great energy, a booming voice, and a superb knowledge of soldiering. He was able to do exactly as Franklin wanted and taught American soldiers to follow orders and complete complicated maneuvers.

Three French officers served the Americans with distinction. First and foremost was the Marquis de Lafayette, a rich young French aristocrat who arrived in America in 1777 when he was just nineteen years old. His father had died fighting the British and Lafayette, who believed in the colonists' fight for freedom, hoped also to avenge his father's death. The king of France was not ready at this time to take sides in the war and he refused to give young Lafayette permission to leave for America. That didn't stop Lafayette, who bought his own ship, *La Victoire*, for the voyage, and himself paid the soldiers who were to come with him. Upon leaving he disguised himself by wearing a black wig over his red hair, and set sail from Spain without even telling his wife, Adrienne, goodbye. From his ship, Lafayette wrote the following to his wife:

The German Baron von Steuben and the French Count de Grasse were among the foreign officers who helped achieve victory at Yorktown in 1781.

CONCLUSION DE LA CAMPAGNE LIBERTÉ DE 1781 EN VIRGINIE.

To his Excellency General Washington this Likeness of his friend.
the Marquess de la Fayette, is humbly dedicated.

By le Mire.

Cette Estampe se vend avec Privilege du Roy à Paris chez le Mire et porte St. Jacques, à côté du Caffé d'Auberteuil No 120.

My dear Heart, It is from far away that I am writing, and added to this cruel distance is the still worse uncertainty as to when I shall have news of you. . . . I shan't send you a diary of the voyage; days follow each other and are all alike. . . . As a defender of Liberty which I adore . . . coming to offer my services to this interesting republic, I am bringing nothing but my genuine good will.

On arrival in Philadelphia, Lafayette wrote a letter to John Hancock, then president of the Continental Congress, asking for two favors. The first was "to serve at my own expense." The second was "to begin my service as a volunteer." Hancock and George Washington paid attention to his unusual request, but after proving himself in battle, Lafayette was named a general to Washington's staff. He and Washington became lifelong friends, and Lafayette named his son George Washington. Lafayette is buried in France, in a grave covered with soil from Bunker Hill.

The king of France eventually sent four well-trained and well-equipped infantry regiments to fight beside the rebels. In addition to these troops, another French patriot who helped the Americans was Count de Rochambeau, a general the French sent to America to help train the inexperienced American soldiers. At sea was Admiral de Grasse, who commanded the French naval force that blocked the harbor at Yorktown and forced Lord Cornwallis to surrender his entire army of 8,000 men to the French and colonial soldiers who had him surrounded.

The inscription below the picture of Lafayette at Yorktown reads, "To his Excellency General Washington this likeness of his friend, the Marquess de la Fayette, is humbly dedicated."

Fall, 1781
Tuesday

The news of the battle of Yorktown confirmed.

Some months since General Washington broke up the camp at White Plains and crossed the Hudson river, passed quietly through the Jerseys and the Province of Pennsylvania, and joined the young Marquis de la Fayette, who commanded a large force at Elk river.

Here they separated the forces, one body sailing for Virginia, the other marching for the same point.

At a place called Chester (I believe in the Province of Pennsylvania), General Washington heard the joyful news of the arrival of twenty-four French ships of the line, under Count de Grasse.

They had an engagement with the enemy under Admiral Graves, in which the French Allies were victors, and left masters of the Bay of Chesapeake.

The whole American force under Washington surrounded the king's troops at Yorktown; they were blockaded by land and water by an army (including French and militia) of 16,000.

The tremendous firing of artillery took the enemy by storm; they could neither rally nor recover. Their batteries and defenses were completely demolished; their guns were silenced, and no hope of relief or way of escape remained.

On the 17th of October, Lord Cornwallis, the British commander of the land forces, proposed a cessation of hostilities, and two days afterwards surrendered; and articles were signed by which the troops, stores, and shipping fell into the hands of General Washington. Thus was the pride of the royal army laid low.

The thanks and praise be to God! We do not dare ascribe it to the strength of an arm of flesh, but to the righteousness of our cause, and to the might and power our great commander hath been endued with from on high.

*After the American victory at Yorktown,
Lord Cornwallis surrenders to General Washington.*

The people are cautious in their expressions, being
surrounded by the British; but their joy is irrepressible
at the good news, though no public demonstration can
be made.

November 5th, 1781
My husband writes most cheeringly. The letter was
brought by a friend of Major Musgrave, who wished

to make inquiries respecting him, and take charge of his effects. The gentleman seemed to have loved him well, and to have appreciated the sweetness and delicacy of his nature. He was much moved at my recital of the Major's sufferings, mental and bodily. We weep, but not for him; he sleepeth well.

A day of public thanksgiving. May the incense of prayer and praise ascend from the altar of my heart!

My honored father participates in the general joy; not for the discomfiture of the British, but from the hope of peace, which his soul loveth, and the healing of discord.

August 10th, 1782

News of Lord North's resignation of the office of Prime Minister, and the forming of a new cabinet, who advise His Majesty to discontinue the war. Glorious news! Heaven grant it may be true. It is certain the war has proved but great loss of life and treasure, without any real gain to English valor, or concession on the part of the Colonies.

Faces of men, women, and children, brighten with expectation of better times. May their hope be not again overclouded! In war there is not a gleam of light to illuminate the darkness. Its practices are adverse to the law of conscience, and lacerating to the feeling heart.

We are ready to shout the paean of victory, to exult afar off in the triumph, and to cheer on the conflict. But could we witness the heart-sickening details, see the loathsome reality, hear the piercing groan, the horrid imprecation, the fiendish laugh, we should "rejoice with trembling," and mourn the necessity, while we return thanks for the victory.

Then let us pause in silence, and while the good angel of our thoughts brings to our recollection the frightful Gorgon-brood of evils which follow in the train

Beacon fires on the cliffs above the Hudson River celebrate the signing of the peace treaty.

of War, pray without ceasing that Peace may come and reign in our land.

April 23, 1783

The cry of peace resounds! The news came today. The children ran from school, dismissed by the teacher, that all might share in the general joy. They are told that some great good has happened, they know not what. The time will come when they will experience and treasure it as the highest favor vouchsafed by a kind Providence. God be praised!

EPILOGUE

THE AMERICAN REVOLUTION ended in Paris, France, September 3, 1783. This action took place not on the battlefield but in a quiet room with the signing of the Treaty of Paris. By this treaty, America emerged from its colonial status, more than doubled its size, and joined the world community.

America's first peacemakers were John Adams, Benjamin Franklin, John Jay, and Henry Laurens. They were named by Congress to negotiate the peace with Great Britain at the end of America's war for independence. These first diplomats were arrayed against the formidable might and entangling alliances of Great Britain, France, and Spain. The major task was to nurture the Franco-American alliance while simultaneously maintaining the interests of their own new nation. The negotiations ended in one of the greatest victories American diplomats have ever been able to achieve. Inexperienced as they were, America's first peacemakers were able to demonstrate to the world that the United States was capable of dealing with some of the most powerful nations of the world. The final peace

PROVISIONS OF THE TREATY OF PARIS, 1783

1. England recognized the United States as a free and independent nation.
2. The United States boundaries became: north to roughly the present boundary line between Canada and the United States; west to the Mississippi River; south to the border between Spanish East and West Florida.
3. The United States was granted certain rights to fish off the coasts of English-controlled Newfoundland and unsettled portions of Nova Scotia, the Magdalen Islands, and Labrador.
4. The British and Americans were to place no legal impediments in the way of the collection of prerevolutionary debts.
5. The United States Congress was to recommend that Loyalist properties be returned.
6. All fighting should cease and English troops leave the United States without taking slaves or other property with them.

treaty was ratified by the United States in Annapolis, Maryland, on January 14, 1784. Three separate copies of the treaty were prepared to make sure that at least one ratified treaty reached Europe safely on the date specified. Actually, two arrived but they were several weeks late. Great Britain decided not to object to the late arrival, and on May 12, 1784, ratifications were exchanged in Paris by Franklin and Jay for the United States and by David Hartley for England.

A year and a half after Congress ratified the Treaty of Paris, Benjamin Franklin wrote to David Hartley saying, "We long have been fellow laborers in the best of all works, the work of peace."

America's first experience with the process of diplomacy relied mainly on the skills of three representatives.

Today, America maintains relations with more than 160 nations and requires the labor of more than 10,000 men and women in implementing its foreign policy.

Following the Treaty of Paris, Britain began evacuating Long Island. Local patriots immediately turned on their Loyalist neighbors. At least fifty-two Loyalist estates were seized and town officials serving the occupation government were subjected to the wrath of the Patriots. Friends of the king were dragged into court and other officials both high and low were fined and forced to leave the area.

In 1784, the legislature disbarred Loyalist lawyers, took the vote away from Loyalists, and also taxed Long Island

An unfinished painting by Benjamin West (1783) shows the American commissioners to the peace negotiations with Great Britain: (from the left) John Jay, John Adams, Benjamin Franklin, Henry Laurens and Franklin's grandson, William Temple Franklin, who served as secretary.

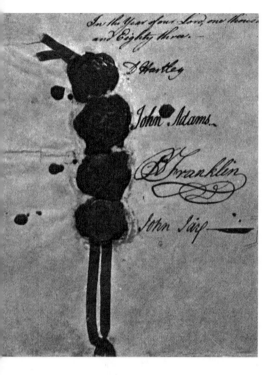

The signatures to the Treaty of Paris

$100,000 "as compensation to the other parts of the state for not having been in a condition to take an active part in the war against the enemy." Not surprisingly, nearly 6,000 Loyalists elected to leave Long Island to settle in Canada because of the unfriendly atmosphere in their home towns. Other Loyalists quietly moved to friendly states such as Maryland to begin again.

The revolution brought many changes to the social and political institutions that once defined Long Island life. Freedom transformed old habits. Elected officials were replaced by newer office holders. The practice of an official holding several offices at the same time was abolished. And family history and economic status were no longer major criteria for holding office.

The revolution similarly affected religion. The Anglican Church, so long associated with Loyalists, went into steep decline when state support vanished and Loyalists emigrated. Religious pluralism grew rapidly and Methodists and Baptists soon achieved parity with Quakers and Anglicans.

With the election of President Washington, Long Island began to take its place in the new republic. Within two decades of the peace treaty, the population boomed, farming grew increasingly commercial, industry, banks, and newspapers sprouted, and fleets of whaling ships sailed

IMPORTANT EVENTS OF THE
AMERICAN REVOLUTIONARY WAR

Date	Place or Event	Victory
Apr. 19, 1775	Lexington/Concord	Am.
June 17, 1775	Battle of Bunker Hill	Br.
July 3, 1775	Washington assumes command of Army	
July 4, 1776	Declaration of Independence	
Aug. 27, 1776	British take Long Island	Br.
Sept. 15, 1776	British occupy New York City	Br.
Oct. 28, 1776	Americans retreat from White Plains, NY	Br.
Dec. 26, 1776	Washington's surprise attack on Hessians at Trenton, NJ	Am.
Jan. 3, 1777	Battle of Princeton, NJ	Am.
Sept. 11, 1777	Battle of Brandywine	Br.
Oct. 17, 1777	Burgoyne's surrender at Saratoga, NY	Am.
Dec. 19, 1777	Winter at Valley Forge, PA	
Feb. 6, 1778	U.S. and France become allies	
June 28, 1778	Battle of Monmouth, NJ	Draw
May 12, 1780	Siege of Charleston, SC	Br.
July 11, 1780	French troops arrive	
Aug. 16, 1780	Battle of Camden, NJ	Br.
Sept. 15, 1781	French fleet drives British from Chesapeake Bay	Am.
Oct. 19, 1781	Cornwallis surrenders at Yorktown, VA	Am.
Sept. 3, 1783	Treaty of Paris signed	

from Long Island harbors for distant oceans. In another ten years Long Island's ox carts, packed earth roads, and sailing ships were replaced by turnpikes, steamboats, and railroads that tied city and country together.

FOR FURTHER READING

Bailyn, Bernard. *Faces of Revoltion: Personalities and Themes In the Struggle for American Independence.* New York: Alfred A. Knopf, 1990.

Bonwick, Colin. *The America Revolution.* Charlottesville: University Press of Virginia, 1991.

DePauw, Linda Grant. *Founding Mothers: Women in America in the Revolutionary War.* Boston: Houghton Mifflin Company, 1975.

Harling, Frederick and Martin Kaufman. *The Ethnic Contribution to the American Revolution.* Massachusetts: Westfield Bicentennial Committee and the Historical Journal of Western Massachusetts, 1976.

Kaplan, Sidney and Emma Nogrady Kaplan. *The Black Presences in the Era of the American Revolution.* Amherst: The University of Massachusetts Press, 1989.

Langguth, A. J. *Patriots: The Men Who Started the American Revolution.* New York: Simon and Schuster, 1988.

Meltzer, Milton. *Benjamin Franklin: The New American.* New York: Franklin Watts, 1988.

————. *George Washington and the Birth of Our Nation.* New York: Franklin Watts, 1986.

————. *Thomas Jefferson: The Revolutionary Aristocrat.* New York: Franklin Watts, 1991.

Morris, Richard B. *The Peacemakers.* New York: Harper & Row, 1965.

Stokesbury, James L. *A Short History of the American Revolution.* New York: William Morris and Co.,Inc. 1991.

Tuchman, Barbara W. *The First Salute.* New York: Alfred A. Knopf, 1988.

INDEX

Numbers in *italics* indicate illustrations.